For Michael,

Your books have influenced my work as a teacher, leader, and learner throughout my career. I am deeply honoured that at this full circle moment in time, you are now reading my first book.

With gratitude,
Carolyn
June, 2021

What Others are Saying About

Renewal

Breathing New Life into School Leadership

"Carolyn Cameron's *Renewal* provides a clarion call to school principals to see their schools with new eyes distanced from the day-to-day routines and open to new possibilities. Drawing on her rich experiences as a school, district and provincial leader, Cameron builds a compelling argument that school leadership cannot be defined by a set of standards for professional practice. Rather, the case studies of Joe, Christine, and Reia point to the complexity of school leadership that is embedded in relationship and grounded in learning. She asks leaders to consider the ways in which they can slow down to be curious observers of their learners—both young and not so young. Rich with poetry from Maya Angelou to Rumi and Emily Dickinson, a strong research base, and practical reflections from school principals, this book creates pictures of possibility for a school system where every learner belongs and succeeds."

> **Judy Halbert EdD,** Transformative Educational Leadership Program, University of British Columbia, Co-author of *Leadership Mindsets:Innovation* and *Learning in the Transformation of Schools and The Spiral of Inquiry: For Equity and Quality.*

"School leadership is entering a new phase—more central, more important than ever, but faced with critical challenges. Energy, commitment, inspiration, and capacity are all required but as Cameron makes clear 'Renewal' is the lifeblood of influential, impactful leadership. Trust and humility and collaboration are essential, but above all to lead a transformation agenda involving people, institutions, and systems you need to renew yourself. Educators, read this book."

"This book is a gift to all educators seeking to create schools with the capacity to change lives—students' and teachers'. Unlike books with simplistic prescriptions and lists of pragmatic steps, this book models the very nature of change in its style and content. The stories here and their wisdom shine light on the complexity of leadership, on the need for and challenges of changing old ways of doing school, and of the very habits, dispositions, and attitudes school leaders should seek to embrace if they are expecting to breathe new life into their schools. Carolyn speaks to leading with soul and presents this remarkable book with genuine humility and authenticity. It's a reading for a future of hope and renewal."

"We've been conditioned as educational leaders to believe that our value is tied to our sense of urgency and to the grandiosity of the projects and tasks we take on and complete. The reality, though, is our impact is most felt in the moments inbetween: the conversations in the hall, the silent nods of understanding, the hope in our smiles, and the genuine empathy in our eyes. In *Renewal*, Dr. Carolyn Cameron embarks on a refreshing departure from overused soundbites that underdeliver and cuts through all the noise to speak the truth about what it really means to lead in our profession."

"Through openly exploring her own leadership experience along with insightful analysis of school leaders in a range of contexts, Cameron uncovers the technical complexity alongside the humanity of school leadership. Offering more than a narrative, Cameron's progression of analysis invites new and experienced leaders alike to take action in the renewal of schools and systems."

Joanne Pitman MEd, Superintendent: School
Improvement, Calgary Board of Education, Alberta

" *'(a) reflective, curious approach to learning-centered leadership recognizes that freedom found in the open, in being open, and in looking for openings is a more responsive, natural way to support and nurture the learning and growth of a school that learns together.'* This quote provides the perfect fertile ground, in which Carolyn plants the seeds of her insightful reflections on responsive and open leadership. Carolyn captures the intangible, natural ebb and flow of a school community, and describes leaders who organically respond to the intricacies and complexities of leading. Carolyn challenges you to revisit and rethink how you lead and to resist the temptation to think inside the box; instead, she asks you to be open to responding to the complex energies that exist in a school. Her personal stories bring to life what the essence of openness in school leadership truly means. A beautifully written book that will inspire you to reflect on your ability to be open as a school leader."

Laurie Kardynal MEd, Assistant Superintendent, St.
Thomas Aquinas Roman Catholic Schools,
Leduc, Alberta

"This book is an insightful and inspirational portrait of school leadership that is grounded in relationships and promotes individual and collective growth. Cameron's use of research, poetry, philosophy, and personal experience prompts deep reflection and invites consideration of current education systems through a more ecological lens that emphasizes the interconnected nature of learning in schools. Her accounts of the joys and struggles of being a principal illustrate both the complexity and the humanity of school leadership."

Julia Rheaume EdD, Associate Dean, School of
Education, Red Deer College, Alberta

"This book uncovers the extraordinary possibilities that are present in the ordinary moments of being together with others in a school community. Cameron's ability to strike a chord of familiarity with the experiences she describes leads the reader to recognize that there is a unity and oneness we all share as we navigate life together with others within the walls of the schoolhouse."

Dianne McConnell PhD, Associate Superintendent, Parkland School Division, Stony Plain, Alberta

"Cameron releases those inner thoughts that lead us toward a renewed model of school leadership that seeks to enhance the learning experience for all. If you have ever yearned to build 'responsive, growth-oriented, adaptive learning communities,' this book is a refreshing perspective, focused on hope and collective action."

Jessie Shirley MEd, Assistant Superintendent, Grande Prairie and District Catholic Schools, Alberta

"As someone who worked with Carolyn Cameron and has benefited from her leadership, I am glad that the insights from her educational journey are documented in this book. With a compelling mix of personal and professional anecdotes, Carolyn also provides practical examples that will push the thinking and the practice of any educational leader. This is a thought-provoking read that will support you no matter where you are on your learning and leading journey."

George Couros, Educational Consultant, Edmonton, Alberta, Author of *The Innovator's Mindset* and *Innovate Inside the Box*

"Renewal…Breathing…New Life. When one considers breathing, there is an in-take of fresh air and an exhalation via a transformative, organic process. Dr. Cameron discusses that, like physical bodies, the best school settings are living systems where continuous learning exists. In these 'living' organisms, one must 'behold the open… where there is no one right way to do the work.' In contrast to stark lock-step, archaic approaches to educational leadership, Cameron believes schools must be 'responsive to the unique individuals'— the learners—be they the students, the teachers, the educational leaders or the policy makers. The ultimate goal is to be open to ways to make learning matter and be relevant. When one is open, we must pause and be reflective to reach a deeper understanding. How can we not be open and connected as 'understanding never occurs in isolation'? As educational leaders, we are helping our school teams prepare students for scenarios in our global world that may not even exist. Dr. Cameron's work is a gift of freedom to explore when we face challenges as co-learners. Be open to multiple possibilities. Let creativity flow like an enthralling poem. Dr. Cameron's work may lead to an exciting renewal in school leadership."

Susan Brannigan-Rampp MEd, Education Leader & Author, Algonquin & Lakeshore Catholic District School Board, Napanee, Ontario

Renewal

*Breathing New Life Into
School Leadership*

By Carolyn Cameron, EdD

Leadership for Learning Network

www.carolyn**cameron**.ca

Renewal: Breathing New Life into School Leadership
Published by
Cameron Leadership for Learning Network
2105, 10136 104 Street NW
Edmonton AB T5J 0B5 Canada
https://carolyncameron.ca

1 0 9 8 7 6 5 4 3 2 1

A copy of this book is retained by Library and Archives Canada.

ISBN Print edition: 978-1-7772107-0-0
ISBN eBook edition: 978-1-7772107-1-7
ISBN Audio edition: 978-1-7772107-2-4

Cover design, interior design and logo by Jordy Kwas | jordy@techyeti.ca

Printed in the United States of America

_____

Cameron Leadership for Learning Network
Tel: +1-780-446-7938
Email: info@carolyncameron.ca

For my new granddaughter, Cooper.

May your joy, your light, and your curiosity become even brighter and more alive as you join a school community that learns together.

Koru

The koru is a symbol resembling the unfurling frond of the native New Zealand silver fern. The circular shape of the koru conveys the idea of perpetual movement while the inner coil suggests a return to the point of origin. It serves as a metaphor for the way in which life both changes and stays the same. Some say that the koru represents harmony. Between the chaos of change and the calm of the everyday, lies a point of equilibrium, a state of harmony in life. The baby silver fern frond slowly unwinds as it grows into maturity. It then opens into a brand-new leaf on the silver fern plant where it ages and then dies. This is the fern's life cycle. It is symbolic of new life, new beginnings, and the hope that is associated with a step into something new and unknown. It is a reflection of the spirit of rejuvenation and growth that comes with undertaking new challenges.

Contents

Foreword

This book is a welcome addition for school principals interested in side-stepping the seemingly relentless calls for increased standardization and surveillance. While there are many books offering remedies in endless checklists on what principals ought to do to improve schools, Cameron offers a different approach. She plays—in a wonderfully hermeneutic manner and an uncommon way—with common dilemmas and choices facing principals.

Weaving her own experiences, along with those of the three principals who participated in her research study, Cameron examines what it means to be wide awake to one's practice. Through carefully woven stories of particular events and experiences, Cameron invites us to look at familiar and taken-for-granted practices in new ways. Providing wayfinding for principal leaders who find themselves at odds with the technicists, she provokes principals to be open to others, to find different ways to be together, and to learn to live the questions.

While this might sound too romanticized, too idealistic for some, Cameron provides sufficient examples to show the practices she asks principals to orient toward require courage, cognitive clarity, and moral fortitude. They are anything but fuzzy or idealistic.

Drawing upon particular instances—moments in time—where wide-awakeness, cognitive clarity, and existential concern come together, Cameron provides glimpses into the alternatives. Using these moments, she reminds the reader of the responsibility of their own choosing, which might be one not readily found in the familiar and well-trodden practices. Choosing the path less trodden, she frequently reminds school principals that choosing is of a moral and ethical nature; it is connected with other people. Failing to cultivate such a connected and interconnected relational stance of wide-awakeness to one's practice, in thought and in action, sets one adrift, to act on impulses of expediency typically grounded in linear, efficiency-seeking solutions to complex problems.

The work principals undertake is inextricably connected with other people: children, the youth of our world, teachers, parents, and the greater community. Recounting the murder of a colleague, a teacher in her school, Cameron shows how a principal must draw upon the roots of moral choosing that lie at the very core of a person's self-concept. As she states, "this time of leadership made me realize clearly that there is no once-and-for-all handbook for school principals." Even a Google search or a hefty filing cabinet could not provide the needed answer. Rather, reaching deeply within herself to find the courage to lead well through this most difficult of circumstances, she chooses "to pay attention to a complex interacting set of living relationships by providing open space for learning, being open to that which is struggling to emerge, and looking for openings to nourish growth."

This book is an invitation to challenge the metaphors and the taken-for-grantedness that underpin many assumptions of what it means to be a school principal. Putting aside "traditional trappings of predictability and control that characterize school settings led by mechanical, lock-step account-ability processes," Cameron invites readers to imagine a more ecological approach to what it means to lead. Drawing upon metaphors from ecology, she shows how matters of diversity, sustainability, and renewal take on new meaning, not as add-ons to the existing system, but as alternatives. Failure to orient toward a more relational, generational, and ecological orientation is captured in the song her son wrote in his last year of high school: "Our Last Year as Cattle." Cameron draws upon her son's experience of schooling to remind all principals of their awesome responsibility to remain wide awake to young people in their midst and to attune them to the endeavor of school-ing in which they participate.

Schools as places of vigor and possibility come from seeing anew, for seeing deeply, interpretatively, hermeneutically. In seeing, hermeneutically one looks to read any particular event in terms of its fullness, its richness in undeveloped, even unseen, potential. When viewed through an orientation toward the ecological, one can create a thriving school community that nurtures individual and collective growth. It is this reality—in all its complexity—that Cameron asks us to accept. She shows us, repeatedly, in chapter after chapter, how this reality can exist in schools through the work that principals undertake.

Sharon Friesen PhD
University of Calgary

Acknowledgments

My gratitude and appreciation run deep for the gifts bestowed upon me from an exceptional circle of colleagues, mentors, family, and friends. Your brilliance, support, inspiration, and guidance have been a source of my continual renewal as an educator and contributed to lighting the way toward completing my first book.

To my *kindred spirits*, the three passionate principals who participated in my study, for their insightful conversations reflecting their deep dedication to teaching, learning, and leadership.

To my inspiring mentor and supervisor, Dr. Sharon Friesen, for her constant presence with me throughout my doctoral journey. Her willingness to "walk the same landscape over and over again no matter how apparently fruitless or painful the steps" provided me with the insight to uncover myself "in ways that remain to me utterly mysterious." (S. Friesen, personal communication, March 30, 2018).

To my multi-age teaching colleagues, long-time friends, and partners in crime, who set out to create different learning experiences for students within a different environment that saw us come together to be with each other differently. You helped me learn there is nothing more powerful than a team with a dream.

To the visionary leaders who contributed to shaping my leadership practice. Your belief in finding better ways to meet the needs of today's learners enabled you to clear the path for my colleagues and I to do school differently.

To Galileo Educational Network, for being critical friends and mentors to my staff and me as we endeavored to make authentic learning a priority at my school for students and staff.

To my incredible school staff and my leadership teams for your willingness to continuously learn and grow together to serve the learning needs of our amazing students.

To my skilled editor and mentor, Dr. Virginia McGowan (McGowan & Co.: The Write Edit Group), for your guidance with my manuscript. I am so grateful to you for early on planting the seed of an idea about writing this book that eventually took root and blossomed.

To my son Brett, for your courageous pursuit of excellence. You demonstrate that you can create opportunities to live the life of your dreams through vision, hard work, and determination. You inspire me to continue chasing mine.

To my son Ryan, who arrived in my life as my own version of Hermes, messenger of the Greek gods. Your messages, hidden within the songs you wrote, the adventures and stories you created, and the struggles you encountered, helped me open up to new ways of seeing and understanding long before I learned about hermeneutics: "The world calls them its singers and poets and artists and storytellers, but they are just people who have never forgotten the way to fairyland" (Montgomery, 1911).

Thank you, Ryan, for creating the crack that allowed the light to get in. You illuminated within me a deeper understanding of what our schools need to be so more people do not forget the way to fairyland. Your brilliant, creative spirit is an inspiration and has served as a constant reminder we can and must do better for *all* of our students.

And to my husband, Jim, who always believes that I can do anything, even when I don't yet believe it of myself. Your confidence in me has caused me to dream bigger, dig deeper, and do better than I ever imagined possible. Thank you for always adventurously chasing the next dream with me. "Write the book! Write the book!" you said. I don't always listen to you; this time, I am really glad I did.

I gratefully acknowledge these publishers for granting permission to reprint:

"On the Pulse of Morning" from ON THE PULSE OF MORNING by Maya Angelou, copyright © 1993 by Maya Angelou. Used by permission of Random House, an imprint and division of Penguin Random House LLC. All rights reserved.

"A Community…" copyright © 2012 by Wendell Berry, from *The Long-Legged House*. Reprinted by permission of Counterpoint Press.

Excerpt(s) from LETTERS TO A YOUNG POET by Rainer Maria Rilke, translated by Stephen Mitchell, translation Copyright © 1984 by Stephen

Introduction

—

Leaving the Old for the New

An Invitation For You

Your presence is requested throughout this book as you join me in a most important conversation about learning, teaching, and leadership.

I invited you because whether you are a teacher, or a leader of teachers, or a leader of leaders, you care deeply about our children and their future in our schools. What I ask of you, as we enter into this dialogue, is not that you agree with what I share. Instead, I ask you to consider what particular insights or experiences strike a chord of familiarity for you. That is your moment, the point in time when you might come to understand something differently, and through that understanding, perhaps something profound might emerge that will make a difference to your unique situation.

Please know that what I share in the pages that follow is not my "expertise." Rather, what I am interested in doing is helping you to see for yourself places in your own work and life where there is something more to think about, something more to discover, so that you might seek to renew your work with and for the learners in your care.

September 1985

Today I open the door to a space I have been imagining for a long time. Today, the dream is about to become real. For four years I studied the educational theorists, psychologists, and behaviorists. I practiced my skills under the guidance of experienced mentors. I learned about curriculum, pedagogy, and current technology of the day (reel to reel film projectors, the opaque projector, and the filmstrip projector!) Now, it is my time to put it all into practice as I welcome students into my first classroom. I am a real TEACHER!

Before my students even set foot into my classroom, I was told stories about them from the others, those who would become my teacher colleagues. These were the students that no one wanted to teach. They did not fit into the standard boxes that defined belonging throughout the other classrooms in the school. My class of fourteen students ranged in age from 12 to 15 years. They were disengaged from learning, lagged in basic skills, and were socially disconnected from their peers. This class of students, identified as the least desirable to teach, was handed over to a bright-eyed, naïve, and optimistic first-year teacher.

They entered my life when I had so much to learn about what matters in the day-to-day practice of building a community of learners. My four years of university "training" did little to prepare me for the reality of teaching and what it means to teach well. These students, and those who followed after, would become my most profound teachers. From my students I knew I would always seek to make learning matter for the kids in my care.

Finding ways to make learning matter for the kids in my care has fueled my passion as an educator; first as a teacher then as a school leader, a teacher of teachers. The kids in my care…they are all so different and so are their teachers. What learning matters to each individual? Oh, how mind numbing is it for leaders, teachers, and students to just *sit and listen*. The implication is that educators intentionally see individual students as just another number, as one of the herd, as though they are all the same; worse yet, they look right through them as though they are invisible.

Unfortunately, this is what the experience of "doing school" feels like for many learners as they move through grade after grade of public school. It is not necessarily the fault of teachers. We have inherited a structured approach to schooling that makes it difficult—if not impossible— to free ourselves from the grip of tightly controlled processes put in place to organize the larger system. What a challenge we face in trying to be more responsive to the unique individuals who enter into the spaces we create for learning.

Ideas about deep engagement in learning that excites, people who support and collaborate, and creating a place where we all feel a deep sense of belonging, do not seem to fit with the rigid structures of a traditional school setting. Yet these ideas continued whispering, as a quiet inner voice, throughout my career. I know these ideas are speaking when they show up as this lived question: *"What if"*?

- What if we could reach this child?
- What if we could help this family?
- What if our schools were places where conditions were created for ALL learners to fall in love with learning?
- What if every school's leadership was organized to more closely resemble networks of influence rather than forces of control?
- What if we became better teachers just by being in our schools; just by elevating each other?
- What if all schools became places where children's natural curiosity for learning was awakened or re-awakened?

Most recently, as I continued to explore these questions more intentionally through my doctoral research, I uncovered the complexity inherent in bringing the collective together to learn from and with each other within the structures of a government-mandated, fragmented curriculum. As in many jurisdictions, Alberta—my province of work and residence—uses a prescriptive form of professional practice standards that attempt to define quality teaching and quality leadership within the public school system.

My study surfaced the tension that exists for leaders committed to enacting leadership for meaningful engagement in learning while also attempting to adhere to strict government-legislated policies. Leaders are caught in the crossfire of bringing forth a new way of being together in schools that is dynamic, adaptable, and responsive while also paying heed to the call for compliance and accountability to fixed, rigid requirements that prescribe what is to be learned and how this is to be done. My lingering questions drove the writing of this book: How might we understand this differently and, with this understanding, open up possibilities for the renewal of our classrooms and schools? How do we create school communities that learn continuously?

As I attempted to answer these questions, a more compelling purpose for this book revealed itself. It is not to uncover one truth, one theory, or one set of instructions to follow that will provide the key to unlock the door to learning, growth, achievement, and success in the role of school leader leading a school that learns continuously. This is impossible. School communities, as living systems, are too complex. When school communities are viewed within the context of a living landscape, learning is understood as a relational, contextualized, and contingent process. Living fields of knowledge are dynamic and emerging against a backdrop of continuous change. No simple recipes or toolkits are available.

With this in mind, my purpose for writing this book is to share the words, the stories, and the experiences for each individual reader to uncover deeper meaning for themselves. It is through this discovery process, unique to each reader, that understanding that transforms rather than merely explains is possible. This is an understanding that recognizes the ever-changing, dynamic nature of experience and our continuously shifting understanding of this experience. It is also an understanding that never occurs in isolation, it is always undertaken in community with others.

I devoted my time, my moments of reflection and my writing to paying attention and using language carefully to describe the rich, multifaceted, nuanced, and relational character of the life of a school leader as it is lived. According to Nancy Moules, a professor in the University of Calgary Faculty of Nursing, and her colleagues:

> It is in the richness of the power of these individual, particular moments of grace, kinship, and human relationship that our human practices have always found their own graceful and powerful place—in the context of one human life, here and now, in this, and this, and this.[1]

The transformation of understanding about leading in complex school communities that awaits the reader in the chapters that follow is significant in so far as it serves as an invitation to do things differently. The education of our children, our most valuable resources for our future, is too important to be reduced to a one-size-fits-all model that stresses accountability and compliance. Learning organizations that respond to the particulars of individuals, to lives led in the presence of others, to knowledge constructed in community, and to the storied nature of complex learning in a complex world, are the possibilities that await a promising future for classrooms, schools, and school districts.

I invite you to journey with me into the living landscape of school leadership in a school community that learns together. In Part One of this book, "Room to Breathe," I draw on inspiration from Rainer Maria Rilke's poem "The Open" as I interrogate our current outdated state of school leadership and the rigidity of contemporary schools. I suggest a shift to a more innately natural way of being together. This shift requires embracing openness and creating space to stimulate authentic learning grounded in a disposition of natural curiosity. It is by orienting toward a more reflective, inquiry stance that openings may be found to create opportunities for deep learning.

Part Two, "Fertile Ground," opens with a favorite poem by Rumi: "A Great Wagon." Rumi illustrates an ideal vision for a space where people come together, "*a field, that grass*," where there is no judgment of each other. It is a moving metaphor for a way of being together that will nurture collaborative learning in a school community that learns from and with one another. Throughout this section, teachers and leaders are called to create the fertile ground needed to make this vision for collective growth a reality.

The final section, "Renewal," begins with the poem "On the Pulse of Morning" by beloved poet Maya Angelou. Angelou provides the direction for this chapter by encouraging readers to open up to an awareness that "*the horizon leans forward, offering you space to place new steps of change.*" This sets the stage for uncovering the concept of change. School settings are living systems and change processes cannot be applied through standardized approaches. I explore what it means for a school community to engage in continuous learning adaptive to a complex, constantly changing context. I suggest cycles of renewal to initiate change as a contrast to the familiar linear approach of continuous improvement processes.

Each chapter begins with a guiding question that sets the direction for the chapter. I intend to provide the reader with a compelling purpose for engaging in thoughtful consideration of what follows. At the end of each chapter, I include a set of reflection questions to deepen the reader's interaction with the subject.

Research and resources are cited throughout the book and are included in the Endnotes and Bibliography. This will provide the reader with an opportunity to locate additional information on the topics.

The book concludes with a call to action that requires leaving the old for the new. By embracing an interdependent, interconnected, and relational approach to school leadership, breathing new life into our classrooms and schools is possible. This call to action would provide a profound sense of belonging for all members of the learning community and allow school communities to respond to dynamic school contexts, while creating engagement in learning that matters. Renewal of this nature moves beyond possibilities and into the realm of reality.

And now, I begin. I hope that those of you who read what follows will go slowly, handle the words gently, and reflect on them deeply so my experiences, the experiences of colleagues, scholars, researchers, poets, philosophers, and students, thoughtfully woven together, might cause you to think differently about teaching, learning, leading, and perhaps even life, itself.

Chi lascia la via vecchia e va per la nuova sa quell che lascia ma non sa quell che trova.

When you leave the old for the new, you know what you are leaving but not what you will find.

- Sicilian Proverb

Thank you for accepting this invitation to purposefully participate in uncovering your own meaning from this book. May it provide opportunities for deep contemplation that call you to action as you continue your work, creating something special for the learners in your care.

Part One

Room to Breathe

With their whole gaze
Animals behold the Open.
Only our eyes
are as though reversed
and set like traps around us,
keeping us inside.
That there is something out there
we know only from the creatures' countenance.

And we: always and everywhere spectators,
turned not towards the Open
but to the stuff of our lives.
It drowns us. We set it in order.
It falls apart. We order it again
and fall apart ourselves.

Who has turned us around like this?
Whatever we do, we are in the posture
of one who is about to depart.
Like a person lingering for a moment on the last hill
where he can see his whole valley
that is how we live, forever
taking our leave.

-Rainer Maria Rilke, The Open

Why are we always in such a hurry?

What does it mean to be turned toward the open? Why are we always and everywhere turned toward *the stuff of our lives*? Most times, it feels as though we have no room to breathe. *It drowns us.* We do not have time to be together differently.

The challenge to making change within our way of leading our schools lies in our fast-paced day-to-day activity-driven workplaces. It is difficult to pause and be reflective or to ask powerful, thoughtful questions that help to create deeper understanding. Too often, government documents dictate what is knowledge and what is truth. Within this structure, there is no need to use valuable, limited time to build new knowledge or seek deeper, conceptual understanding. The rigidly imposed school-year calendar, the artificial boxes placed around students who are sorted and processed based on date of birth, the fragmented school timetable that organizes learning into 30- or 45-minute blocks…All speak to a model of school design that values efficient use of limited time.

Manic pace is cultivated as a virtue in elementary schools. Teachers getting kids to run from place to place, activity to activity. All noise and no sounds. Quiet is under-valued as only the quiet of straight rows—made to be quiet by somebody, not being quiet.

**- David Jardine,
Educational Researcher**

Educational researcher David Jardine reflects on this all too common experience of "frenetic, disconnected fragmented images and free-floating meanings, a twirling free play of signs and signifiers and surfaces, none of which requires or deserves our attention, none of which has a strong or vital link to any other fragment."[2] *The stuff of our lives* can take over. *Who has turned us around like this?* Jardine suggests that what we need is space and time for deeper reflection to connect thoughts, people, ideas, and concepts to something deeper. I used to describe this as "getting off the hamster wheel" of activity, of doing, to create space for being, being open, being curious, being reflective.

It is challenging to slow down the pace of a school. Despite having "so much to do and so little time," I used to carve out precious moments to be with my school community in both formal and informal situations. One of my favorite ways of getting into the mix of school life was to sit on the benches that lined the hallways of the school and watch the people traffic go by. Everyone was rushing to get to the next place. Every once and a while, a student or a teacher would sit down beside me and engage in a conversation. I learned so much about the learners in my school by taking up this practice.

How can we slow down to be curious observers of our learners, both our students and the teachers who create the learning environments in every classroom? How might we take time to look for important clues and evidence we are moving in the right direction and not just spinning our wheels? To begin this uncovering of a different leadership for learning—one open to possibilities for looking at learning and leading differently—I suggest a leadership model that creates room to breathe. This reflective, curious approach to learning-centered leadership recognizes that freedom found in the open, in being open and in looking for openings, is a more responsive, natural way to support and nurture the learning and growth of a school community that learns together: one adaptive to changing contexts.

Chapter One

Behold the Open

Some things you have to let happen organically. That's kind of the magic that comes out of the work we do.

- Christine, School Principal

What if we released ourselves from traditions and structures that no longer work for today's changing contexts?

Today I am not opening any doors. I am walking into my tiny office cubicle. I have no door! Instead, partitions break the workspace up into isolated stations. We can't talk in these spaces; it would disrupt others in their cubicles. This place feels REALLY different. No schools or classrooms are anywhere nearby for me to spend time in.

I am seconded to a position within the Leadership Excellence Branch at Alberta Education. Few educators are in my area of the office building. In the cubicle beside me, investigators pour through files of information collected about a school district leader who was removed from his position and charged with misconduct.

I miss my school district! I question my decision to leave the school system and join the rank and file at the ivory tower of government. I once asked my superintendent what I needed to do to be more effective in my role. He told me I needed to be more political. Well, here I am, about to become immersed in the political world of the Department of Education. I would learn first hand more about the policy makers and the stakeholder groups who contribute to decisions about the system and its learners. I would learn about the red tape of bureaucracy. I accepted this new role with the belief I might contribute to the work our government is doing in building school and district leadership capacity. We expect that the minister of education will approve new quality standards for not only our teachers in the province, but also for our school and district leaders. I suspect they believe these standards will have some impact on the misconduct cases they are dealing with.

I am also in the third year of my doctoral program. I am excited to be conducting my research this year. I will be interviewing three principals from my school district. During my time as a division principal in my school district, I could be in all the schools within my district. I walked beside teachers, principals, and students. I participated in team meetings with teachers, I stepped into classrooms to join the students in their learning and I met with various leadership teams from the schools. I attempted to support their work in creating schools that learn together.

Through these experiences, I took particular interest in three principals: Reia, Christine, and Joe. They stood out for me. I wanted to learn more from them. These three principals focused on student learning by activating leaders and teachers as resources for each other. These school leaders were establishing a collective responsibility to move the entire group forward together as an interconnected community. This way of leading was not widespread *in schools across the district. How could it be? This way of leading did not feel safe and did not conform to following lock-step processes and procedures that are predictable, efficient, and tightly controlled. Safety exists in doing what you are told and, in that safety, perhaps some discomfort in sterilizing the learning experiences of the students, the individuals whose voices often go unheard.*

The issue is to recognize that public schools are not evolving from an outdated, traditional, factory-model approach to one that attends to students' learning in response to new developments and research on learning, the changing needs of today's learners, and changing societal needs. My doctoral research explored this problem by taking a deep dive into the lived experiences of three school principals, former colleagues. They are leading their schools in ways responsive to newer understanding and research about how we learn and how to create a school community that learns together. Their insights reminded me of my own lived experience as a school principal. Their voices triggered memories and important insights that led me to uncover meaning in the way they spoke about their teachers; it revealed the promise in how they worked with their teachers to respond to the incredible complexity that defines today's schools and classrooms.

These lengthy interviews were profound and moving experiences for me. The words of my colleagues reminded me of the intensely draining, challenging, unpredictable, and joyful moments of school leadership. I wondered why their words were evoking such a powerful response from me. Was I still missing the experience of leading a school community? Did their words illuminate old memories previously hidden within me? It was during these deeply reflective moments, which extended into the months that followed these interviews, when memories I had buried and long forgotten were illuminated. I was in the thick of things again! I was in the mess! This time, however, my vantage point was different. This time, I had a view not just from the perspective of a school principal and a district principal given the opportunity to work with principals inside their schools across 22 sites. Now my perspective had broadened to embrace a provincial outlook as my recent work with the government involved meetings with several superintendent teams from across the province of Alberta.

My new role at the time of this research was as educational consultant for the Leadership Excellence Branch. It was this branch within the government's Department of Education that was responsible for the development of and decisions related to the rollout of the province's new Leadership Quality Standard and the Leadership Development Programs. These initiatives would lead to policy requiring every principal and superintendent in the province to be certificated.

I worried. Did this most recent job implicate me as a co-conspirator with the government? Would I be held responsible for tightening the grip of control on our school and district leaders by seeking to enforce yet another standardization process, a process expecting compliance to the "cattle drive" that required checking off more boxes, jumping through more hoops? Or was this a silver-bullet solution that would lead to guaranteeing a better way for our youth to learn?

What has turned me around like this? Do I have evidence of committing this crime on my hands, as a seconded principal with the Department of Education, or did my lone voice get heard when I asked, time and time again, what does this policy, this document, do to build leadership capacity? How would we know our leaders are moving forward as they enact the interconnected competencies they need to develop over time? How are they engaging in the work, solving complex problems, and looking for evidence of impact of their actions as leaders who create the conditions for teachers and students to learn?

Was my newly-added responsibility as a member of the Assurance Review Committee a sign I was being heard? Did they pay heed to my questions about who will lead the work? How can the government and the public be assured that leaders were enacting the competencies in the new standards? Would there be evidence that conditions were being created to support student learning for all? What evidence could be pointed to that would provide the government and the public with the necessary assurance?

Parent, teacher, principal, district principal, Alberta Education consultant, and now, researcher: these roles provide me with an interesting vantage point. I surely was right in this mess, trying to understand the complexities of leadership at a school level, when there is so much confusion to sort out. How could any lone school principal ever hope to get it right? What can be done to make sense of all this? Books have been written, research conducted, and yet a quiet voice from inside told me that my research, my experiences would matter. It was from here I might attempt to untangle the ambiguity and tension inherent in becoming a principal who creates a school community that learns together. In doing this, I could provide insight and support to teachers and leaders in their learning how to lead schools differently.

A Topic Uncovered

In my role as researcher, I poured over transcripts, my reflective journal, and my literature review—reading, re-reading, thinking, re-thinking—to engage in the interpretative process of understanding the experience of my research participants. The first topic that addressed me emerged from my conversation with Christine, a school principal leading a kindergarten through grade nine school.

Christine described how she lets things happen organically; she said, "Magic comes out of the work we do." Her words evoked images of nature, growth, unexpected surprises, and curious occurrences—strange words to use when describing a traditional institutional setting, i.e., that of a tightly-organized school, monitored for evidence of standardized compliance and quality control. Christine's words caught my attention. I wrote them in my reflective journal, starred and highlighted them, and they practically leaped from the pages of my transcripts when I read them over.

Something here needed to be uncovered. What does it mean to let things happen *organically* in a school? What kind of *magic* happens when there are tasks to be completed, curriculum outcomes to be implemented, and marks to be assigned? All within a tightly-controlled system with a prescribed curriculum, expectations for accountability, and professional practice standards for teachers and leaders that set out clear competencies and indicators for success—a cookbook for how to make one a competent teacher or leader. Within this structure, how could a leader possibly lead a school community in a natural, organic way?

The principals I interviewed all spoke to this way of *being* in their schools. What they described summoned powerful and painful memories associated with an experience that called upon a natural, organic way of being a school leader. It was how I survived the most challenging time in my career. I came face-to-face with how to be a leader who leads learning, adapts to change, and seeks to continuously improve by dealing with complex problems and situations. The incident surfaced during my interview for a secondment position with the provincial education department, Alberta Education, that I will describe shortly. After reflecting on that experience, given what the principals in my study shared with me, I realized what Christine's phrase "some things you have to let happen organically" might mean, and how this would help shine a light on the mysterious, complex, experience of leading a community that learns.

What the three principals described throughout their interviews for my research was *openness*. They spoke of a way of being *open* to learning that emerges within the context of the day-to-day experience of school life. Initially, I learned this important lesson during a time in my leadership, when everything I thought I knew about my responsibility as a leader of a school community was literally thrown out the window. What I was called to do, instead, was be open—daily, minute-by-minute—to what came my way: what problem needed to be addressed next and what crisis I needed to attend to, all while trying to keep the learning of our students at the forefront. This memory helped me to bring deeper meaning to what the principals were describing during our interviews.

The ways of being open that addressed me as I listened to the voices of my three colleagues reminded me of policies and processes that blocked our way of being together in a community that learns. Isolation, efficiency, and control were the order of the day as Frederick Winslow Taylor's Management Theory (1911)[3] took hold of educational institutions during the industrial era. His lasting legacy left most leaders confined rigidly to unquestioningly follow a top-down authority model, requiring that they continue to lead through structure, management, compliance, and control. *There is no room to breathe.*

My three colleagues and I did not march to the beat of that drum in leading our schools. We carried out our work in a more open, responsive way, looking for natural moments—*openings*—to create space for authentic learning for both students and their teachers. This meant a shift from being a manager to a learner who leads other learners. It required a disposition of being an observer, a listener: to find a way in, an opening, with an individual teacher or student. All four of us found ourselves swimming upstream as we attempted to break from the status quo of the traditional trappings of predictability and control that characterize school settings led by mechanical, lock-step accountability processes.

Leadership in an open, more natural organic context recognizes the complexity and unpredictability of socially connected individuals within communities. Within a new ecological metaphor, leadership of a school is adaptive. It responds to the contexts in which openings occur for authentic, purposeful learning and leads to intellectual engagement. Learners, students, teachers, and leaders who engage in this meaningful learning experience an energy and passion in their work. A natural, slower rhythm and flow emerges when a different way of being together in community is valued. Within this open space were limiting, controlling, and worn-out processes serving a past that no longer exits, that need to be replaced with new ways of coming together to create excitement and curiosity for the challenging process of continuous learning.

An Unexpected Arrival

During my interview for the secondment position with the Leadership Excellence Branch at Alberta Education, I was asked this question: "What has been the most challenging situation you faced as a principal?" It was an appropriate question. I was being interviewed for a position that would involve assisting with creation of a framework for provincial leadership development programs leading to certification of Alberta principals. It was important that I identified challenges to provide a new perspective on the work of school leader.

My answer came quickly. It was the easiest question I have ever been asked. I immediately recalled a specific time in my career when I questioned whether I had the "right stuff" to make it as a school principal. I responded confidently to the question: it occurred when a teacher was murdered. Awkward moment. Silence overtook the room. Really, how did I expect the panel to respond to my answer?

The question the interview panel asked next haunted me throughout the year when I was preparing for my doctoral candidacy exam and moving forward with my research. Later, as I dove into the interpretive process of reading and re-reading the interview transcripts, my literature review, new leads, and sources of additional understanding, I continued to reflect on how I might have answered the next interview question more insightfully. The question silenced me. In that moment, I was caught off guard. I struggled to answer what appeared to be a simple-enough question. But on that day, the question triggered a flood of memories. I found it difficult to find the right words to talk about one incident in my career that had affected me so profoundly. The question posed was "What learning from that experience could you share with aspiring leaders in a leadership development program?"

What learning? What learning!! How could I capture the heart-wrenching, life-changing learning that emerged through the experience of leading a school community following the horrific tragedy of a murdered teacher?!

I was silenced. I did not know what to say. If I could, even to this day, weave together meaning from the experiences of that time in my career to provide a definitive answer, I think I would be a profoundly wise sage—or an extremely naïve fool. No simple explanation is possible. How can there be? This experience opened up a deeper understanding of the complexities of my role as a school principal, as a person who wished to create a school community that learns together.

> It is truly a great cosmic paradox that one of the best teachers in all of life turns out to be death.
>
> **- Michael A. Singer, Author**

> Things aren't all so tangible and sayable as people would usually have us believe; most experiences are unsayable, they happen in a space that no word has ever entered, and more unsayable than all other things are works of art, those mysterious existences, whose life endures beside our own small, transitory life.
>
> **- Rainer Marie Rilke, Poet**

The only words I could find to say in that moment during the interview were: "I guess I would want future leaders to know that the work of being a leader is not always predictable; *unexpected things arrive*." I do not know how that feeble answer could have possibly impressed anyone on the interview panel, but I got the job.

Looking back, as I continue to follow my desire to provide mentorship, guidance, research, and practical experience to those dedicated teachers interested in leading the learning of others, I have much more to contribute to the conversation. I now know that trying to capture the moments of reflection, awakening, and growth that came out of that lived experience would be impossible to achieve in the brief opening of time available during a job interview. After so much time spent researching and experiencing this complex topic of leading a school community that learns together, how could I ever think that I, alone, might create a special recipe to be followed, a tool kit to be downloaded, that would ensure successful leadership while navigating the sea of turbulence and unpredictability that exists within every school community? It might well take a lifetime to speak about the *mysterious existence* of a school leader to be understandable to those in that interview room. It requires being open to what comes to meet you, and it is becoming clearer in this process that what might be needed is an aesthetic appreciation of one's self being *present* within the role, similar to the aesthetic appreciation for a work of art. This aesthetic appreciation for intense experience is often difficult, if not impossible to put into words. However, the philosopher Gadamer points out that intense experience is not beyond words; it is a matter of finding the right words.[4]

So, my task begins. I gathered insights, dialogue, quotes, poetry from principals, researchers, poets, philosophers, and scholars so that together we might find the right words for understanding the unsayable, mysterious experience of leading a school community that learns. It will be a challenging and collaborative endeavor. I recognize that understanding never occurs in isolation; it is always undertaken in community with others. This is the work of a team with multiple voices, backgrounds, and experiences who will nourish the growth of a deeper understanding about what it means to be a leader who wishes to create a school community that learns together.

Through an unexpected trek into the dark valley of the most difficult time in my career I was awakened to the mystery, the magic, and the miracle of the everyday ordinariness of being a school principal. Facing the loss of a most treasured teacher ignited from within me the strength to keep on with my passion of leading learning and learning alongside of my teachers. *She* was one of our school community's most keen learners. Losing *her* reminded me of how very unpredictable life is, how important it is to stay open to what is before us in the present moment and to find grace in every crazy, chaotic situation we find ourselves in, because, when we bump up against these times in our lives, there is something profound to be learned.

I have a better answer to that interview question now than I had then. Time, space, and reflection equipped me not with a guidebook or a tool kit for describing the work of a principal but, instead, with a compass that keeps my eyes pointed outward, toward the Open, and what I might discover as I open up to whatever comes to meet me in this journey with others.

Back to my interview question: *what did I learn that would help other leaders?* I learned to slow down; to create space for conversation; to listen, with an open heart and an open mind; to believe in the resiliency of our students, of our staff. I learned how powerful a team can be when we stick together and lift each other up. Lyrical poet Rainer Maria Rilke tells us *"With their whole gaze/Animals behold the Open"*; to me, the message is clear. We learn how to open ourselves to each other; we learn about how a living, learning school community organically adapts to changing circumstances. I learned about the magic that emerges from giving people the freedom to heal in their own way, the freedom to connect with others, and the freedom to learn what they need so they can climb out of the valley, stronger and more resilient.

My school community was shaken to the core. Our teacher was taken from us so suddenly, so tragically. We were broken; a crack appeared. But I could not let us fall apart. We needed to stay connected to each other, to our students, to the learning. Through this crack the light got in; we pulled together, we did not fall apart. I opened up to learning that cannot be covered in a how-to book, from a list of leadership guidelines, or from an internet search. This learning was uncovered from experience and, from that experience, a path through the tangled mess opened up. We found our way through. Most of all, I learned to turn my eyes outward and *behold the Open*—the space where there is no one right way to do the work, only an open space to be and become—guided by intuition, presence, and a sense of being exactly where you are meant to be

Marching Forward Through the Mess

This time of leadership made me realize clearly there is no once-and-for-all handbook for school principals. The way I needed to be, the work we needed to do that year, was not information I could Google on the internet or retrieve from my files. It required deep relational work. I needed to be present for things that arrived, for police who came by to question staff members, for parents who came to report information that might lead police in a new direction, to grieving students, to the emotional break down of staff members, and to a new reality for our school that existed under the black cloud of an unsolved murder hanging heavy over our heads. I needed to pay attention to a complex interacting set of living relationships by providing open space for learning, being open to that which is struggling to emerge, and looking for openings to nourish growth.

It was difficult, particularly given external demands for how I should be moving through this time of crisis with my staff. Red-flag reminders were provided regularly about making sure my staff was not grieving too much or becoming too dependent on me. I needed to keep them marching forward through this mess so they could march the students forward. Keep the human assembly line moving. Do not be too human; do not let them see your grief, your confusion, your worry, and do not slip up—this is a murder investigation. All eyes are on you and your school community. I needed to be strong and support the teachers but also keep a close eye on the learning of the students and be available to listen to any leads or information that students, families, and staff were sharing that might warrant a call to the police to assist their investigation.

Most important, I needed to determine if teachers were doing the right work: were the students learning? The learning was not happening in some pockets and places; a few teachers were falling apart and I needed to make changes. Was I becoming a soldier? March on, soldier. Do not buckle under the pressure to keep the assembly line moving. Do not sacrifice the learning of the students for anything. What learning matters, especially for my grade 9 students, who just lost their teacher? They had looped from grade 8 to grade 9 with her. And then they lost a second teacher in grade 9. The size of the loss became too much and a medical leave was taken. Now two of the three grade 9 teachers were gone. Make sure these grade 9 students are ready to write the tests and get the marks. The high school will be sorting them into their grade 10 boxes.

Meanwhile, I was called on to keep my own wall up. No one could see how this was for me. I could not reveal weakness, emotion, or a lack of confidence. There would be no crack in me, no illumination into my inner world of grief, loss, responsibility, burden, loneliness. Brave soldier, battle worn, I marched forward, confident and composed on the outside and ready to break down on the inside. I delivered the eulogy at her funeral without a tear. They needed a strong leader right now. I supported every teacher at the funeral; they were the honor guards for over 1,000 mourning friends, family members, and students. So many tears and raw emotions, but none from me.

At school in the weeks that followed, the students wanted to host a school-wide celebration for their teacher. I agreed and we opened our doors to former students, now in high school; the police were undercover among us looking at the faces and interactions among the guests at this event. There might be a clue to the murderer; the murderer was likely among us. Brave soldier: be strong for your teachers. Keep the students safe. Is the murderer among us? I could not crack under the pressure of this mess.

Nobody knew the toll it was taking on me except for one teacher; she knew. It was Hallowe'en when this teacher glimpsed my inner world. She was bringing her children by my house to trick-or-treat. In past years, I was excited to see my teachers and their kids as they made special trips to my house so I could see their children all dressed up in their costumes. This Hallowe'en was different. It had been only two weeks since the murder. My husband answered the door when the trick-or-treaters came to the house this year. When my teacher asked for me, my husband let her in on the secret. The wall came down with these words: Carolyn had a tough day at school today. She needs some time for herself. This teacher later shared with me she had no idea how difficult this tragedy must be for me, as the leader of our school community. This one teacher now saw through my act. I had none of this figured out.

We must never feel we are alone in taking on the responsibility for leading a school community. Colleagues, friends, kindred spirits are in the mess with us. The burden is enormous. It can never be the work of one lone warrior. The well-being, safety, and learning of all the students and staff is on our shoulders. But there are other brave school soldiers who have had their own challenges to face. They have had crises, mixed messages about the expectations required from them, disgruntled community members, and external pressures for accountability and compliance. Yet, those who are intentional about creating conditions for teacher and student learning march on through challenges and obstacles. They do not turn away from the Open: the place where a new way to be and learn together might be found.

"Behold the Open," admonishes Rainier Maria Rilke. This awakens in me a recognition of something more vast, expansive, and unlimiting to consider when exploring schooling in our postmodern world. What would schools be like for our learners, the children, and those who teach them, if we turned our gaze outward, toward the Open, to explore how to break free of old habits and routines that no longer serve us? To assume the social setting of a school can be led using a one-size-fits-all approach is ridiculous, especially during uncertain times of crisis. There must be a better way.

What Keeps us Turned Around Like This?

"The stuff of our lives", as Rainer Maria Rilke reminds us, has taken us over with ways of *doing* we inherited from times past. Our practices are informed by working traditions we take on unquestioningly. We know this phrase all too well: "This is the way things have always been done." The fragmented and isolated tasks, the factory-line metaphor for traditional schooling handed down to us by those who came before, leaves us drowning in a sea of disconnected bits: "the stuff."

This "stuff" includes the mechanistic structures that are Taylor's legacy. The echoes of Taylor's predictable, results-driven system for efficient task completion still haunts our education system. Indeed, Taylor's scientific management protocol infected all aspects of societal life in the early part of the twentieth century. Our education system is still entangled among these roots.

There is a saying in education: "Old paradigms don't die; they just go to the hospital and get fitted with a cardiac pacemaker. After that they live on with other paradigms, side by side."[5] Today, as previously, decisions of the day, including school reform, are driven by overarching concern for efficiency, conservation to reduce waste, and modern business methods. The way forward was seen to be the application of business methods designed for efficiency in a factory. Under this paradigm, classroom management is viewed as a business problem, with unquestioned "obedience" as the first rule of efficient service.

Before this time, educators conceived of themselves as scholars; after 1910, when Taylor's business orientation took over as the driving influence for success, curriculum was thought to need a more practical focus. The goal was to produce a work force trained for the demands of an industrial society. This approach included an emphasis on developing a scientific understanding about how to break tasks into fragmented, specialized bits to be completed by highly-trained individuals in a more time-efficient manner. This business model, when applied to school settings, required administrators demonstrate they were operating schools efficiently and ensuring the love of learning should not overshadow the power of earning.

Examples of specific features of this management model still with us in schools today are the value placed on measurement and the timely, compliant completion of tasks. It was the belief—and still is today—that workers, similar to students in school, are most effective when given a definite task to do within a given time for a short period only. Clearly, the current fragmented structure of a school day into periods or classes that sees students marching forward from one disconnected topic to the next when the bell sounds strikes a familiar chord with the factory-line model prevalent in the industrial-era workplace. The curriculum is most commonly built on this fragmentation foundation and has not changed since first designed as a scope and sequence curriculum. Outcomes are not connected, ideas are not connected, subjects are not connected, and grades are not connected.

Tightly-managed, conforming, and standardized mechanisms for compliance and control are not a valued process for change and growth in today's fast-paced, diverse knowledge society. But still, we cannot seem to shake these entrenched traditions that bind us to a past that no longer serves us. The old paradigm did not die; it lives alongside the new in a tangled web of contradictions. Added to the mix are the well-meaning efforts of those who followed. Unfortunately, their contributions often reinforce what Taylor put in place.

Edward Lee Thorndike is another key player in the landscape of our Canadian education system whose "influence in Can-

The Law of Effect

The most enduring of Thorndike's laws, the law of effect stated that an animal that made a response in a situation that was followed by satisfaction would be more likely to repeat that response in that situation. Conversely, an animal would be less likely to repeat responses made in a situation if those responses were followed by discomfort.

- B.B. Galef, Psychologist

ada stemmed from his work on human intelligence, mental testing, classroom grouping, and retardation."[6] Traces of Thorndike's laws are still embedded in the culture of modern day educational practices. Thorndike's law of effect—combined with his law of exercise (all things being equal, results in improved connections between situations and responses through repetition)—explained all learning as behavior. In short, as educational researchers Sharon Friesen and David Jardine note, "the effects of reward and punishment and of repetition carried out on the members of any species could yield laws of a general psychology of learning."[7] Remnants from this behavioral approach of reward, punishment, and repetition can be found in classrooms and schools to this day as evidenced by the sticker charts, incentive programs, detention rooms, drill, and practice worksheets that support the school's efforts to manage and control student learning. Keep those students marching forward; the human assembly line must achieve results.

Added to this convoluted concoction are the contributions of Swiss Jean Piaget, who studied childhood development. He attempted to interrupt behaviorism, stating people did not learn through reward and reinforcement. Rather, Piaget maintained that people learned by making sense of experience themselves. Piaget's legacy of constructivism described how individuals each make sense of the world by picturing knowledge as applying a sense of order to the confusing nature of experience.

Piaget maintained that the learner is central to making sense of the complex nature of discovering patterns and disciplines of knowledge for themselves. Friesen and Jardine describe Piaget's contribution:

Piagetism presumes that what comes to meet you is chaotic and contextless and his work simply adds into this mix an active agent—each child constructing his or her own knowledge out of the fragmented bits. Given that knowledge is understood to be thus "constructed" out of isolated, disassembled fragments whose relations to each other have been erased, teachers lose track of how to interrupt students' constructions without simply imposing their own constructions. Recourse to the interrelated, living discipline that houses such fragments has been cut off as a way to proceed. Since the alternatives are now teacher constructions or student constructions, classrooms become student-centered, students become left to their own devices. Such efforts are important and well-meaning. After all, there is a hint here of trying to put the initiative and involvement of individual students, which Taylorism had effaced, back into the educational mix. However, if the presumption of curriculum as constituted by isolated fragments is left in place, such efforts eventually collapse and such student-centeredness becomes replaced with its seeming opposite: teacher-centered classrooms or variations on "back to the basics."[8]

Trying to order and re-order the mess is what we experience as normal. Attempts to interrupt or change this "normal" experience are inordinately difficult. For a principal who works in ways with teachers that call into question schooling still weighted down by the legacy gifted by Taylor, Thorndike, and others enchanted by the call for efficiency, a re-orientation to new metaphors for schooling is needed.

Natural Moments

A new future is struggling to emerge from the legacies of our past. New voices are ready to shape what it means to enter into *the Open* spaces for learning. These new voices suggest an organic, ecological orientation to understand what it means to learn together. Lifting the voices of the principals provides a hint of this new metaphor for the learning of teachers in their schools. As Christine states, *"Some things you have to let happen organically. That's kind of the magic that comes out of the work we do."*

Magic: this word caught my attention. The word magic can be traced back to the late fourteenth century word *magike*. It was described as the art of influencing events and producing marvels using hidden natural forces.[9] The magic and mystery

Sometimes in those natural moments, I find it the least threatening to teachers. They don't feel like they're being judged, they don't feel like they're being criticized about something they're doing.

When you can capitalize on those moments, which I think can reshape the relationship dynamic in a way where it's about two colleagues collaborating, learning from one another to improve our own practice which will improve student learning. I think those natural moment are some of the most powerful moments. When I saw a change in people's practices, it often came from those natural moments.

- Joe, School Principal

associated with hidden natural forces describes the nature of life itself. What we understand as knowledge and the truth of a matter unfolds as something mysterious and magical. Our understanding is always contingent and constantly emerging; it shifts, changes, and refuses to be pinned down. A thread of mystery and magic runs through the fabric of life lived and understood through inquiry and interpretation. As my dialogue with the principals unfolded an understanding of the magic nature of learning continued to grow.

My interview with Joe, the principal of a K-6 elementary school, provided me with insight into the value of natural moments. *Natural* is a thirteenth-century word that means of one's inborn character; hereditary, by birth.[10] It is in a teacher's inborn character to care deeply about their students. Perhaps this is why, when a teacher cannot succeed in nurturing student learning, that a way in to the teacher's private world of teaching can be found. The child who is not learning creates a crack in the wall, an opening for Joe to meet the teacher around a particular moment, a practice, a child. As Joe stated in the previous quote, "Sometimes in those natural moments, I find it the least threatening to teachers [because] they don't feel like they're being judged, they don't feel like they're being criticized about something they're doing."

Joe emphasized these natural moments are a way to break down the structures and formal processes—those embedded in Taylor's lasting legacy— that hinder entry into dialogue around how to understand what might be done to help that particular child. The natural, as referred to here, seems to resonate with living, interacting relationships.

Joe maintained what Elliot Eisner, a leading professor of art and education at Stanford University, called the "complex interacting set of living relationships" between himself and his teachers as those that require attention.[11] Joe suggested the emergence of new learning that starts with intention, his intention, to know what he believes should be happening between teachers and students, and the organic nature of taking opportunities that arise in the day-to-day practice of his work for

> Put as simply as possible, school improvement—and therefore the improvement of education for students—requires attention to a complex, interacting set of living relationships. Ecology is perhaps the best metaphor that I can use to characterize these living, interacting relationships.
>
> **- Elliot Eisner, Professor of Art and Education**

the authentic learning of his teachers to occur. Joe identified the connectedness necessary when engaging in learning conversations with his teachers. He raised the concern that learning, for his teachers, cannot occur in fragmented bits taken out of context. Knowledge, people, and organizations as living systems are highly complex and adaptive to change. This ecological conception illustrates the interactions within complex living systems, including social organizations like classrooms and schools. Through an ecological lens, terms such as living, organic, and evolutionary can describe the characteristics of a complex adaptive system.[12]

The Open might be further conceived of as a place where change is embraced, creative potentials are unleashed, and new learning is a source of freedom from doing what we have always done—a welcome change from traditional ways of structuring or controlling the learning in our schools. This perspective of change would allow for the potential of new opportunities to be released and would endlessly inspire curiosity, thus creating an organization focused on learning.[13]

What Joe described speaks of one who sees himself as someone who guides teachers to question their taken-for-granted practice. He notices things that come up naturally within the day-to-day practice of his teachers and initiates learning conversations through questioning. In this way, Joe is supporting a learning environment with his teachers that is "constantly perturbating and being perturbated" as educational researchers Brent Davis and Dennis Sumara observe.[14] Teachers are being encouraged to trigger thoughts about new possibilities for their instructional practice in *the Open* space of a community that learns together.

> So framed, the teacher is not only another learner within the classroom, but an integral part(icipant) within a grander learning system. Along with all the other individuals, the clusters of individuals… and the classroom collective as a whole, the teacher is teaching/learning. The teacher, that is, is constantly perturbating and being perturbated within the evolving, self-prompting system of the classroom collective.
>
> **- Brent Davis and Dennis Sumara, Educational Researchers**

For Reflection

Chapter One: Behold the Open

1. What remnants of the industrial model of education exist within your context? What needs to remain? What needs to be renewed? What is standing in the way of making change?

2. What are some of the most challenging experiences you have had as a leadership team? As a teaching team? How did you navigate your way through these challenges? What did you learn from the process?

3. What is the shared vision for student learning within your school community? For teacher learning? For principal and district leader learning? For superintendent learning? What evidence do you point to that tells you this vision is being lived out?

4. How might existing policies, including curriculum renewal, be adapted to meet current research on learning and building teacher and leadership capacity within today's dynamic classroom, school and district contexts?

Chapter Two

Being Open

I just don't think there is a magical prescriptive way of how you shape learning in your building. I think it needs to come from an inquiry base.

- Reia, School Principal

What if we were open to seeing learning in our classrooms and schools through a different lens?

April 2006

Today I opened my office door and I picked up the phone. It was the high school calling again…about my oldest son, Ryan. No, he is not absent today. He's here at school, but he showed up late. Phew, that was a relief. Ryan has missed so much school this grade 12 year. I was constantly being informed about Ryan's absences through the automated attendance system. This time, I was actually talking to a real person. That's nice, for a change, I thought. "We think he's been drinking. We need you to come and meet with us."

What????!!!! I dashed out of my office inside the nearby middle school where I was working as an assistant principal—as a leader in our school system. How could this be? We have a good home, we value education, we try to be good parents, we love our son, we support him, and we will do anything for him. He's brilliant, sensitive, creative; he has everything going for him. Doesn't this high school see that? What is WRONG with him? Why does he hate school so much? Is it the school? Is it us? Is it him?

As I drove the short distance between my school and his school, these thoughts flooded my mind. I arrived to meet with the team. The counselor, the assistant principal, Ryan, my husband, and I, sat around a table. They talked about my son like he was invisible, looked right through him; just sit and listen, sit and listen. They told us that the traditional school environment is not where Ryan will do his best learning. He had accumulated too many absences and, today, he showed up under the influence of alcohol. It was time for him to do his learning elsewhere. He doesn't belong here.

OH MY GOD! I AM A FAILURE! I have failed my son as a mom, as a teacher, as a school leader. My son is getting kicked out of high school, with only a few months until grade 12 graduation. No questions asked. No discussion to figure out what we should do, as a team, to help him. No support for the family. Oh, but they did have a plan: the standard plan for any student who does not follow the attendance rules here at high school. Ryan is to attend the outreach school for the remainder of the year to graduate—independent study packages; read and regurgitate. No problem, he has been doing that for several years now.

What happened here? My brilliant, curious, talented son, the one creating artwork and writing stories well before his peers in kindergarten, had his writing published in early elementary school, won the district's speech arts competition in junior high school, topped his class in his Language Arts Provincial Achievement Test in grade nine with a perfect score, performed music he had written himself at school-wide assemblies. This bright light was not welcome at school anymore. What had gone so wrong that a system intended to open doors to new opportunities, prepare our future generation to become the thought leaders, artists, musicians, entrepreneurs, community-minded citizens and lifelong learners had failed my son. Or had we, as busy parents caught up in our day-to-day routines of work, kids' activities, doing, doing, doing the next thing, failed our son? Or, had my son simply failed to thrive in the system? What needs to change? Is the system designed to engage ALL learners in learning that matters to them? These questions have become deeply personal.

Before the structured, regimented routines of school life, my sons, like many pre-schoolers, were exposed to countless opportunities to explore the world around them, create adventures, travel, question the people and places they were exposed to, and live life in an authentic, curious way. My sons, like many other children who enter the school system as curious learners, slowly but surely lost their spark of wonder after each passing year in an institution that seemed intent on structuring their learning into de-contextualized, often irrelevant, disconnected chunks of content dissemination. An institution where individual interests, student voice, and responsiveness to the uniqueness of each learner was not always a priority. Streamlined, efficient processes that push many students through, what often feels like, an impersonal system that sorts individuals by age rather than skills, dispositions or interests. These processes were, and still are, seen as the most efficient way to ensure quality control of the masses. A specific example of one student's disillusionment with the system came when my son, Ryan—a creative musician, songwriter, and recording artist—upon beginning his grade 12 year of high school wrote a song entitled "Our Last Year as Cattle."

The words from my son's song title "Our Last Year as Cattle" haunt me still, as I wonder about what is needed to break free from the cattle drive of compliance and control that our system has inherited from the past and continues to impose on today's learners.

A school community aspiring to create a way of learning together orienting to *the Open* would not want students—or the teachers who teach them—feeling like cattle compliantly moving from class to class, in-service to in-service, disconnected learning bit to next disconnected learning bit; becoming skillful at playing the game of getting educated; passing the tests; writing up the year plan or the professional growth plan for "the boss"; following the rules of the game; and counting down the days until they are released to participate in real life outside the walls of the school.

Being Curious

Many have contributed to a conception of the learning that would resemble the authentic world that exists beyond the structured, controlled classroom environment. For students, authentic learning experiences would more closely mirror the complex tasks that occur in life. This type of learning would include active construction of knowledge that uses students' prior knowledge, expands on learning through dialogue, and engages learners in disciplined inquiry over a sustained period. In addition, this learning would seek to match the real-world tasks of professionals, have assessment woven throughout, be influenced by the context in which it takes place, and create a sense of community by building on the knowledge and ideas of others.

This *lifeworthy learning* is, as Harvard education professor David Perkins observes, "likely to matter in the lives learners are likely to live."[15] Being open to authentic learning places value on curiosity as a guiding, foundational principle in the design of tasks. Would this same design of authentic learning for teachers allow them to also engage as curious learners having their own authentic learning experiences?

Unfortunately, it is all too common to experience a loss of wonder, curiosity, and imagination upon entry into the system of education. One of my son's favorite childhood tales, *Peter Pan*, reminds us of the unfortunate fate of those Lost Boys who left Neverland to begin a new adventure.

> Of course, all the boys went to school; and most of them got into Class III, but Slightly was put first into Class IV and then into Class V. Class I is the top class. Before they had attended school a week, they saw what goats they had been not to remain on the island; but it was too late now, and soon they settled down to being as ordinary as you or me or Jenkins minor. It is sad to have to say that the power to fly gradually left them.[16]

What way of being would be needed to lead a school community, a classroom community that does not steal from learners, students, and the teachers who teach them, their *power to fly*? Reia, the principal of a kindergarten through grade nine school, reminds us that meaningful learning cannot be prescriptive. Authentic learning is not a tightly-controlled, managed endeavor.

All three principals from my study spoke of the learning of their teachers as requiring an openness to what emerges during the day-to-day experiences of the classroom and school. It requires freedom to explore the stirrings awakened in the natural moments of the work.

Uncovering the look of openness in a classroom experience begins when a question worthy of the time and attention of the classroom community arrives. This requires a certain disposition on behalf of the teacher: to remain open to opportunities that arrive for a particular group of students in a particular moment that makes learning a memorable experience. Educators Pat Clifford and Susan Marinucci highlight that the arrival of a question that the community of learners investigates together,

demand[s] that understanding develops in a public space in which each person's abilities, interests, perspectives, and talents help move everyone else's thinking forward. It is a knowledge-building space in which ideas are at the center, and each individual has a commitment to producing the collective, evolving understanding.[17]

A teacher who is able to explore his/her own freedom may be the only kind of teacher who can arouse young persons to go in search of their own.

**- Maxine Greene,
Educational Philosopher**

To listen carefully and openly to the question being posed means the teacher needs to be prepared to linger over the question to determine whether it is worthy of rest and repose—worthy of returning to and whiling over. Teachers who engage their students in being open to the question have spent time cultivating things worthwhile. It is within such a classroom that learning is understood as questions that lead to other questions, and in probing, debating, and seeking answers, a sense of wonder and curiosity is invoked and genuine intellectual engagement is nurtured. I remember a time when two of my teachers exploded into my office with such excitement about the unexpected arrival of a topic of study that had hooked their learners. They stumbled across the topic, the tragedy of 9/11, from their work with a novel they were exploring during their language arts classes. They wanted to address this as a research topic that would fit in with the study of worldviews from the social studies curriculum. They were keen to uncover with their students how worldviews changed after the events of 9/11.

What followed from the conversation I had with these two teachers was the design of a powerful time of learning for students and teachers. Two classes of grade eight students dove into research around the events from 9/11 to prepare for Socratic Circles. In the Socratic Circles, they engaged in dialogue with each other that would help them uncover the deeper meaning of the effect that 9/11 had on shaping their individual views and the worldviews of others.

The teachers described the excited conversation that students entered into daily as they explored this topic. And it did not stop with classroom learning; students, almost all, went home each night to continue reading and learning more about the events and the perspectives that were a part of this important time in our history.

The topic arrived, unexpectedly, and teachers were open to its arrival. Teachers connected what was, for students, a worthwhile topic to the curriculum they were expected to teach. We worked through how they could design this learning, together, to build on the momentum created by a topic that mattered to their students.

The same can be said of principals who lead the learning of their teachers. The principals all spoke about being open to the authentic learning of their teachers: learning that arises simply out of a question that addresses them. Being open is not a task to complete or an activity to participate in. It

Intentionally, with walkthroughs, what I do is shoot a quick email back after I've been in a walkthrough that celebrates an area of the TQS. If I have further questions or concerns, I don't put that in writing. I just ask them to check in with me. I want to learn more about something.

When they check in with me, I will then celebrate something that I saw, and then say, "okay, tell me a little bit more about this," because my impression of "this," once I've had a chance to really listen to what their intention was, where they were going with it might be different than what I thought on my own.

If I'm still concerned, then I can question, ask a little bit more, and then offer a strategy. Sometimes after that clarity, there's no longer a concern there.

- Reia, School Principal

is a disposition that requires a way of being in the school, not as the expert, but as a co-learner with teachers, clusters of individuals, and the classroom collective: being open to new opportunities to learn together.

Reia spoke to her intentional practice of seeking to observe specific knowledge, skills, and attitudes outlined in the Alberta Teaching Quality Standard (TQS) as she engages in growth and learning conversations with her teachers. While she provides guidance and feedback to her teachers, she also shared her practice of being open to uncovering misconceptions about what she was noticing in her teachers' practices. Reia understood the complex nature of pedagogical practice and welcomed opportunities to engage in dialogue that will make teacher intentions explicit and provide a shared understanding of her teachers' experiences.

Reia described the opportunities that conversation and listening open up for the learning of teachers and her own learning in understanding their work more deeply so she is in a better position to ask the next right question. This relational work takes time and a willingness to enter into shared moments of reflection and dialogue together.

Being with People

Is there a toolkit that teaches one how to *be with people*? Standards for teachers and leaders exist. They prescribe the competencies and indicators that one would expect to see in the practice of a competent teacher or leader; however, having a guide does not necessarily equip one with the disposition needed to enter into shared dialogue as co-learners. This disposition seeks to build knowledge together to improve student learning.

What does it mean to walk alongside others and be open to moments when opportunities for conversation and learning present themselves? These questions lead to an understanding that the principal or the teacher, in deciding in the moment-to-moment experience of teaching and learning, are engaged in the practice of interpretation. In this way they become curious inquirers into the unexpected discoveries that catch their attention and cause their understanding to, as hermeneutics scholar Nancy J. Moules and her colleagues describe, "waver and tremble."[18] The principal and teachers are deciding about what they notice from the practical experiences of teaching and learning and how their background knowledge of a particular teaching methodology or approach might support the practice of their teachers: not as an imposition upon them, but as an opportunity to open up the dialogue about practice.

The German philosopher Hans-Georg Gadamer discusses the importance of keeping open the space of practice as an act of human responsiveness. This experience resides in the openness of the space between being and becoming. The voyage into this space "permits us to learn, to see differently, and, thereby to extend our horizons", explains his advocate, philosopher Nicholas Davey.[19] Reia spoke to this space and created a process of interpretive inquiry into the practice of her teachers. She displayed the disposition of being open to the conversation and what her teachers shared with her to create a different way of understanding their teaching practice.

Being open requires a distancing process that allows one to become a curious observer, not open but still tied to their own subjective experience, knowledge, and understanding of the topic. Being open requires, writes Davey, "the skill of being critically distant while remaining involved, attentive, and caring."[20]

New voices contributing to the dialogue on being open come from the ideas and teachings of spiritual thought leaders. In his fictional account of the journey to awakening from his book *The Celestine Prophecy*, James Redfield describes being open:

We must take an observer position. When a thought comes, we must ask why? Why did this particular thought come now? How does it relate to my life questions? Taking this observer position helps us release our need to control everything. It places us in the flow of evolution.[21]

Author John Muth combined his studies of Zen, a school of Buddhism strongly influenced by Taoism, with his love for the Russian novelist, philosopher, and social reformer, Leo Tolstoy, to create a simple but profound storybook titled *The Three Questions* based on Tolstoy's writings. This book—about compassion, living in the moment, and fulfilling our purpose for being— poses three questions:

1. When is the best time to do things?
2. Who is the most important one?
3. What is the right thing to do?

What Muth uncovered through this story is an insightful reminder of the living relationships that need attention in the work of leading a school community that learns together. The guiding compass for this complex understanding reflects the simplicity that can be found in eastern spiritual traditions:

> Remember then that there is only one important time, and that time is now. The most important one is always the one you are with. And the most important thing is to do good for the one who is standing at your side. For these, my dear boy, are the answers to what is most important in this world.[22]

Muth's simple message provided further support for the relational work of leading a school community that learns. The three principals shared experiences that provided insight into their intention to have one conversation at a time with their teachers as they uncovered problems of practice or opportunities to celebrate successes together: in naturally occurring situations, in this moment, at this time.

Taking the stance of a curious observer, entering into genuine inquiry about the practice of teaching requires a stepping back. As Joe described, "it's about two colleagues collaborating, learning from one another to improve our own practice and improve student learning."

Learning together this way involves participation in the world in a co-evolution of the knower and the known that transforms both and allows for a shift in thinking that moves away from the notion of learning as mechanical, fragmented, and content delivery, and moves toward a more organic, emerging, and open approach. Learning from this perspective, Davis and his colleagues propose,

> is no longer seen as a process of 'taking things in' but of adapting ones' actions to ever-changing circumstances. This view of learning recognizes that it is an evolutionary process and as such, is neither linear nor driven

by competition or selection. Instead, it is creative; it influences and is influenced by a 'dynamic and evolving landscape of possibility'.[23]

Classrooms and schools, as living ecologies, are full of unexpected challenges and surprises. They offer opportunities for making new discoveries at every turn as the unique contributions of students, teachers, and leaders in a dynamic state of being and becoming, continuously evolve and co-evolve among an interconnected context, shaped by tradition, experience, and change. Eisner suggests being open to the unknown means being open to opportunities to learn and grow within authentic contexts, opening "new paradigms for understanding how we learn make it challenging to deliver a teacher-proof curricula or the use of a check-off observation schedule for evaluating teaching or a Betty Crocker recipe for advancing teaching effectiveness."[24] While educators are handed a one-size-fits-all curriculum from their government, the one size does not fit all, nor is one size needed to guide effective teaching. Curricula and learning are far more complex, requiring an openness to the learner and the subject at hand and a reflective, curious openness to discovering unexpected surprises that will contribute to new understandings.

Stepping back, detaching, and becoming an observer of learning creates a way of being open that allows entry into genuine inquiry. It requires child-like curiosity and a commitment "to stop doing and stop knowing in order to start asking."[25] Teachers with a curious disposition become activators of student learning. They not only become learners themselves, but also see learning through the eyes of their students.

I made many attempts to create time and space for teachers and students to engage in connected, deeper learning experiences. We established looping processes that enabled teachers to spend more than one year with their students, so they could extend the time needed to know and understand their learners. We blew up the traditional junior high timetable in favor of creating longer chunks of time for students to remain with their teams of teachers. We created weekly chunks of time for teachers to collaborate around the design of learning for their students. This was an attempt to slow things down to create deeper, more connected learning experiences for both students and their teachers.

Christine described what she did to slow things down for her teachers. For her, it meant taking things off her teachers' plates.

The balance is what can you do so people don't feel overwhelmed? What can we take off their plates? What can we start to just adapt instead of always saying you should be doing more, change, and be doing more? And I've always been a fan of you can never force professional development. You can show that things need to change in a certain way because the decision is based on data. So something like the nature-based program started with a very passionate few people and then the goodness just leaked out, right. So when they see it with their own eyes and they're going, "Oh I could adapt that to what I'm doing already."

Perhaps what Christine is alluding to is the balance achieved by not necessarily removing something from the plate but of finding a way to create a unity or wholeness that integrates all the disconnected, isolated bits and bites teachers have on their plates.

It started off as two or three teachers very passionate about wellness in nature-based programming and so we now have after school sessions that the teachers are organizing; we have kids spending an hour outside every day doing their mathematics and science and even in the winter. It's amazing.

Some things you can be really intentional about, the mathematics is an example. We've been watching those results for years but some things sort of just come up because it's part of what everybody is talking about anyway.

Worry about anxiety and depression, lack of attention and then how it ties in with a solution such as becoming more nature focused is fascinating because that one just organically happened and now it's become huge.

- Christine, School Principal

Being in Flow

Researcher, spiritual teacher, and author Michael Singer offers this contribution on being open to flow to maximize the energy available within an interconnected community:

The more you learn to stay open, the more energy can flow into you. You practice opening by not closing. Any time you start to close, ask yourself whether you really want to cut off the energy flow. Because if you want, you can learn to stay open no matter what happens in this world. You just make a commitment to explore your capacity for receiving unlimited energy. What you'll find is that the only thing you really want from life is to feel enthusiasm, joy, and love.[26]

All three leaders in my study described enthusiastically the energy flow created from new learning that is authentically pursued by staff members. The enthusiastic accounts of unexpected learning teachers experienced shared a common feature: they all occurred when leaders let go of control and opened up the space for teachers to step, together, into the flow of learning. A sweet spot of energizing, engaging learning happens when boredom or stress gives way to genuine intellectual engagement.[27] The learning of teachers is propelled to new levels of excitement and enthusiasm when they feel supported to build their skills and knowledge around a topic that matters to them. Christine shared the "fascinating" growth that took off when she provided the support for an initiative that "just organically happened and now it's become huge." It was driven by a topic that interested her teachers and one which was worthy of their time and attention. Christine's own fascination with the topic contributed to the collective energy created and the contagious passion spreading outward throughout her school community.

That group checked in with us frequently to see if where they were going was what we, as leaders, had wanted. We just kept saying to them, "We don't have an end in mind. We just know we want a rich journey that's so connected to curriculum and authentic."

I think there were probably two kids out of 70 that did it at an "adequate level." For everybody else, the learning was astronomical; but what my assistant principal and I did was anytime we were able to attend the alternative professional development with teachers, it was the questioning that we would provide around the table that I think helped push some of the validation of certain things that they were doing, as well as question some of the things they thought were either going well or not well.

- Reia, School Principal

Joe spoke about his teachers being in flow of learning when given free-dom to experience different ways of working with their students: "People need to be free to try different things." He provided support in time and exposure to other possibilities. Embedded in his description is his attention to being non-judgmental while celebrating efforts to engage in learning, even if the efforts don't always result in success: "creating these learning opportunities that fill people's buckets, not take away and expose them to something else." His attention and focus were centered on the process of his teachers' learning rather than the product.

Reia's teachers embarked on their own authentic learning experience by being given the opportunity to discover, for themselves, the way they want-ed to design learning for their students. Reia outlined general expectations, but she trusted her teachers to deepen their own understanding by applying their skills and knowledge to their task. However, she did not abandon her responsibility to support their learning along the way. She described how both she and her assistant principal learned alongside of the teachers, being mindful to not manage or control their learning but, instead, ask the right questions that would provide guidance and an opportunity to reflect on their work. She described with enthusiasm the learning for students that resulted was "astronomical."

All three leaders shared their experiences as curious co-learners, learning alongside their teachers, inquiring into their practice. These leaders described how they helped to design challenging, yet engaging, learning for their teach-ers by creating conditions for flow experiences. This way of being together is underpinned by an insightful pre-understanding that one principal described:

> Everybody wants to do well. Every child, every staff member. I just sometimes think we're not making it explicitly clear what some of our goals are and we're not being intentional enough when we're noticing it's not there. How do we figure this out together? How do I help you so that you're not overwhelmed?

Reia's words hint to a shift in the relationship dynamic: one which sees the leader becoming a co-learner and a coach who believes in the competence and strengths of all learners who strive to ask the right questions, scaffold the learning, and look for openings to initiate learning conversations.

For Reflection

Chapter Two: Being Open

1. In what ways are you providing authentic learning experiences for your students? To the staff? To school and district leaders?

2. How do you engage in open dialogue with colleagues? With your staff? How do you decide when and where this will happen? Are colleagues engaging in open dialogue with each other?

3. In what ways are you providing time and space for staff to engage in open dialogue about their professional practice?

4. How can you, as a teacher, a principal, or a district leader create time and space for learning conversations with your colleagues?

5. Can you describe times when staff felt energized by their learning? What processes were in place to support this? How were you involved in this learning?

6. How are parents engaging with staff in open dialogue about learning?

Chapter Three

———

Openings

...clearing of things into the mystery beneath...[Is] a process by which things emerge from concealment into unconcealment.

- John Caputo, Philosopher

What if we looked at problems as openings that allow us to breathe new life into our schools?

Philosopher John Caputo's idea of openings is echoed in the lyrics of singer-songwriter Leonard Cohen[28]: Cohen reminds us about cracks being places where the light gets in. Illumination is created, bringing the light of new understanding to what might first appear as a troubling or difficult situation: a crack. This apt metaphor describes how we can learn to understand problems differently. This chapter will linger over an opening—the crack through which the light gets in—as an opportunity for the discovery of authentic learning.

Quality Control or Authentic Learning for Teachers?

From my conversations with leaders and the research I explored, I will now take up finding an authentic opportunity or passage that will allow leaders access into the inner life-world of teachers and their practice. This is a different approach to that which has been traditionally understood about instructional leadership. The term instructional leadership was described early on as the technical skills of coordination and control required to align the school's academic mission with strategies and action. The instructional leader's responsibility was to focus not only on leading but also on managing. The school principal, as the sole leader, carried out managerial tasks that included coordinating, controlling, and supervising curriculum and instruction. The role of the principal, as an instructional leader, placed a focus on the control of teaching (i.e., evaluation) rather than on its development.[29]

The leadership model developed by instructionally-effective schools requires a strategic plan for improvement by coordinating the school goals with the curriculum. In this context, instructionally-effective leaders need to be able to use data to inform decisions. More recently, an instructional leadership model has re-emerged in response to the call for higher academic standards and accountability. The underlying concern of this new model of instructional leadership is that it is difficult to implement the new accountability practices at the center of this data-driven decision-making model.[30] Clearly, the emphasis on results and one-size-fits-all data to measure success does not align with a model that seeks to look inside itself and its own school context to imagine and create new ways of learning and being together. With external accountability bringing pressure to perform, leaders are hard-pressed to explore new and unchartered territories of qualitative, observational, and reflective practices with their staff.

The tightly-controlled, monitored, and evaluative concept of instructional leadership has perpetuated the fragmented, mechanistic approach to teacher learning in a way similar to what has been described as the industrialized model for student learning. This description provokes images of teachers complying with the external drivers for their performance. They feel judged on their ability to jump through hoops set out for them as opposed to being authentically engaged in learning that will make a difference for their students in this classroom, on this day. Most orientations to leadership—which are intended to be supportive of teachers in their efforts to grow stronger teaching practices—are cast in instrumental terms by many who have contributed to the research literature on instructional leadership. Tracing instructional leadership's history reveals reliance on technical approaches that will lead to the growth and learning of teachers. The term *instructional leadership* emerged from "Effective Schools" research in the 1980s. It was based on the finding summarized in a collection on keeping good teachers: "in effective schools, principals focused on student and teacher learning and on monitoring progress and achieving key instructional objectives."[31]

Educational researcher Michael Fullan believes that principals need to go beyond instructional leadership to build new cultures based on trusting relationships and a culture of disciplined inquiry and action. This would be a departure from what Fullan defines as *direct* instructional leadership: principal actions that directly affect instruction as evidenced through a tighter, more prescriptive approach to observing and reporting back to teachers based on more systematic, fragmented supervision routines for principals and their teachers.[32] Others suggest "the facilitation of learning and growth should be the number one responsibility of an education leader."[33] The focus of the work of instructional leadership should be growth-oriented toward instructional support "that seeks to improve learning, teaching and shared instructional leadership," say educational researcher Jim Brandon and his colleagues.[34] This support work happens in the day-to-day experiences of teachers.

Finding a Way In

The principals in my study hinted at the contextual learning of their teachers being important by recognizing the cracks that their teachers shared as portals, or authentic openings, allow them to enter into dialogue, share understanding, and illuminate possibilities to explore to improve practice that led to improved student learning.

The openings present themselves in the day-to-day context of the work. For these leaders—who are intentional about being present and open to emerging problems of practice—they are opportunities to open up teaching practice and enter into dialogue. This, in turn, leads to deeper understanding for improved practice within authentic contexts of their work. Joe described it this way: "capitalizing on these moments, creating these learning opportunities that fill people's buckets, not take away and expose them to something else."

Leading the learning involves a new understanding of what it means to learn. Living the landscape of learning describes learning to live in the environment, the unique contexts within the space where the subject disciplines naturally exist and are part of larger networks of connection. The open space for learning, being open, and openings speak of learning that is different: understanding what it means to hold vision, attitudes, and action in an ecologically, organic, natural way; recognizing the interconnectedness of learners and learning; taking place within a dynamic living field, wherein leaders are present and open to authentic learning—authentic learning that opens up in natural moments of the day-to-day experience of teaching and learning within complex school communities. Such an organic,

> You get at talking about curriculum and instructional practices and assessment through talking about individual children. Because that's what they want to talk about. We spent a whole half an hour talking to a teacher with the whole team of counselors and learning coaches and administrators, etcetera, about a particular child; but what ends up coming out of that meeting is not just a think tank about that child and what's the action plan and what are we going to do for that child. It's hugely about instructional practices.
>
> **- Christine, School Principal**

ecological approach to learning is a challenging shift in thinking, doing, and being in schools. Eckhart Tolle, author of *A New Earth*, captures it this way:

When we go into a forest that has not been interfered with by man, our thinking mind will see only disorder and chaos all around us. It won't even be able to differentiate between life (good) and death (bad) anymore since everywhere new life grows out of rotting and decaying matter. Only if we are still enough inside and the noise of thinking subsides can we become aware that there is a hidden harmony here, a sacredness, a higher order in which everything has its perfect place and could not be other than what it is and the way it is. The mind is more comfortable in a landscaped park because it has been planned through thought; it has not grown organically. There is an order here that the mind can understand. In the forest, there is an incomprehensible order that to the mind looks like chaos. It is beyond the mental categories of good and bad. You cannot understand it through thought, but you can sense it when you let go of thought, become still and alert, and don't try to understand or explain. Only then can you be aware of the sacredness of the forest. As soon as you sense that hidden harmony, that sacredness, you realize you are not separate from it, and when you realize that, you become a conscious participant in it. In this way, nature can help you become realigned with the wholeness of life.[35]

Tolle challenges us to realign with the wholeness of life. This way of thinking about things does not begin with isolated bits and pieces but with webs of relationships not simply comprised of individual things but constitutive of them. The web of relationships provides a wholeness to experience teaching and learning of students, their teachers, and their leaders. This wholeness is available to us when we turn our gaze outward and find room to breathe in the Open—the space where there is no one right way to do the work, only an open space to be and become. It is here where we can be awakened by the surprises and mysteries that lead us to new ways of understanding and where openings allow us a way inside, to grow and evolve as a school community that learns together.

For Reflection

Chapter Three: Openings

1. Can you recall a time when you engaged in powerful learning with your staff based on a specific problem they were experiencing within their own context? What did you do to move learning forward?

2. What do you do to be present within the learning context of your staff members?

3. How do you engage staff, students, and families in strategic planning for your school community? In what ways does this planning allow for flexibility and responsiveness to the unexpected arrival of new learning or a change of direction?

4. In what ways do you blend formal evaluations of staff members with informal, formative observations and conversations for growth?

Part Two

Fertile Ground

You breathe; new shapes appear,
and the music of a desire as widespread
as Spring begins to move
like a great wagon.
Drive slowly.
Some of us walking alongside
are lame!

Today, like every other day, we wake up empty
and frightened. Don't open the door to the study
and begin reading. Take down a musical instrument.
Let the beauty we love be what we do.
There are hundreds of ways to kneel and kiss the ground.

Out beyond ideas of wrongdoing and rightdoing,
there is a field. I'll meet you there.
When the soul lies down in that grass,
the world is too full to talk about.
Ideas, language, even the phrase each other
doesn't make any sense.

The breeze at dawn has secrets to tell you.
Don't go back to sleep.
You must ask for what you really want.
Don't go back to sleep.
People are going back and forth across the doorsill
Where the two worlds touch.
The door is round and open.
Don't go back to sleep.

-Rumi, A Great Wagon

What are the conditions for growth that support an organization that learns together?

The language in this poem creates a vivid image: "a field," "that grass", an open space to meet together "out beyond ideas of wrongdoing and rightdoing": no judgments, no preconceived notions of wrongness or rightness. The words "each other" take on new meaning. Perhaps it is us together finding a wholeness that replaces our disintegrated relationships. Where is that "field"? How do we cultivate that space where "the soul lies down in that grass"? How do we awaken to a new way of being together in our schools? Is this even possible? Or do we continue to enter onto a battlefield of *my way versus your way*, with rutted routines and structures holding teachers and principals in place, where every step in a new direction feels like a call to engage in an all-out war: a war waged for freedom to do what is natural—engage our children's curious minds.

Fertilis means "bearing in abundance, fruitful, or productive" and is derived from ferre: "to bear."[36] This etymological tracing of the word fertile sheds light on the need for fertile ground that is fecund and lush as a necessary condition to establish a culture within a school community oriented toward growth. Once again, a turn to using an ecological metaphor to understand a school community that learns together is a reminder that when a fertile, productive environment is available, a natural flow of learning opportunities exists. It is within this context of living, interconnected relationships where an abundance of new growth in learning is possible.

Leaders who wish to create the conditions needed for a learning culture to take root do not do this using an easy-to-follow recipe: first do this, add a little of that, next step, mix in more of this. In a complex social setting, nothing is that simple. Rather, what is called for is a constantly evolving and dynamic process. Qualitative researcher Ruthellen Josselson reminds us it is a dance that requires leaders stay open to all possible aspects of the dance; hearing both the music and the words.[37] The leader who creates fertile ground must be simultaneously attentive and understanding.

The burden of ensuring growth for all learners, including the teachers, rests on the shoulders of this attentive gardener, the leader of learning. Thích Nhất Hạnh, Vietnamese Thiền Buddhist monk and peace activist, advises that as an attentive gardener, the leader must understand "When you plant lettuce, if it does not grow well, you don't blame the lettuce. You look for reasons it is not doing well. It may need fertilizer, or more water, or less sun. You never blame the lettuce."[38]

This topic of creating fertile ground for learning together provides an imagery in sharp contrast to the traditional structure and prescribed standardization associated associated with the industrialized model for schools and what it means to get educated. Within this new ecological metaphor, learning is not forced or controlled; it is cultivated. Leaders who aspire to this model of school leadership must, obviously, recognize the inherent risks in making a shift from compliance and control through their positional authority to a more complex, vulnerable position: that of being a participant in the learning process with their teachers. Creating safe spaces where people can learn together, where individuals feel valued for who they are and what they can contribute to the community, create the fertile ground within a school community that learns together.

Chapter Four

A Different Way to Be Together

Let's sleep the day away
We agree that there's something in the air
You're such good company
Let's just remain here
Give me back those days
Show me the words and show me the ways to feel it
Start filling it up for me and I could be so brave
I could be so brave
Without this mind I'd be so brave

- My son, Ryan, "Brave"

What if we walked beside each other to nurture growth and learning?

"Let's just remain here"; my son's song lyrics echo a longing to hold onto the present and the comfortable. It takes courage to awaken from routines and familiar ways of knowing, doing, and being as an educator. Challenges arise in supporting teachers to enter community with each other and push their own and each others' learning as they shift toward creating a culture of learning in each of their schools.

Exposing yourself to others, sharing what you know and what you do not know, flaws and all, takes bravery and an ability to make yourself vulnerable to colleagues. Rumi referred to the shared human experience of fear in his poem "A Great Wagon": *Today, like every other day, we wake up empty and frightened.* It takes courage to awaken to a way of being with others that is authentic, that makes one vulnerable to the exposure of not having it all figured out. As Rumi admonished us: *Do not go back to sleep. You must ask for what you really want. Do not go back to sleep.*

Christine provides the fertile ground, creating the culture for her teachers to explore professional learning communities. This school identifies itself as one already excellent and not necessarily in need of learning or growing to continually improve. Teachers rarely opened the doors to their classrooms and working collaboratively was not an accepted practice when she arrived as principal. She explored opportunities for teachers to pilot professional learning communities.

"I feel so supported; I enjoy coming to work every day. I feel like there's no dumb question for the group, there's a sense of trust." That's what I heard from the pilot group. It built such a sense of trust amongst five or six adults who have more in common than they know and they found that out right when they chose a topic. And even a couple would say, "You know, I couldn't believe that my colleagues didn't understand, you know what I mean?"

It should start with children's learning but we know that that's human nature to protect self first and then to look beyond self.

- Christine, School Principal

Exposed!

Summoning the courage to bravely expose gaps where new learning and growth are needed is challenging. The challenge is far less daunting when there is a culture of learning established within the school community.

Trust. Christine's comments caused me to consider the concept of trust. When she said, "No dumb question...I couldn't believe that my colleagues didn't understand...[and took the stance to] protect self first," I was struck by something profound. It is incredibly difficult for teachers and principals to risk being exposed for not being the experts they believe they are expected to be. It is impossible to be a learner open to growth and change if we work within a culture that places judgment on each other for not knowing something.

> Struggles are mostly working with staff who have the opinion that, "I've got this. I've got it. I know what I'm doing." And we always try to seek first to understand. Is that coming from a place of confidence, or is that coming from a place of insecurity?
>
> **- Reia, School Principal**

Christine described the culture that her pilot group created with each other: a culture that suspended judgment regarding questions. The words "protect self" is an insight into why teachers and principals are reluctant to open themselves up to learning. A critical element of trust is required for an individual to feel empowered within a community. It is an empowered individual who is brave enough to take risks; all learning involves risks.

Educational researchers have found that the act of engaging in learning together as a collective community involves risk. The risk taking required to open up to new learning is impossible if schools cannot create conditions for safety and trust. School communities where leaders ensure relational trust is built can support the authentic learning and continuous growth of the learning organization.[39]

Vulnerability. A community built on trust possesses the humility to recognize that everyone, from the leader, to the teacher, to the student, is a learner. Among adult learners, this means that learning is nurtured in open spaces where individuals come together to collectively improve the learning for students. Leaders who model openness to new learning create the fertile ground required to nurture growth for all learners in their schools. The challenge that exists in this brave, bold approach to leadership cannot be overlooked. It can feel much safer to rely on positional authority requiring strict compliance to policies that prescribe a single truth with one way to teach and one way to lead.

Leaders who intentionally model the risk taking for learning they expect from their teachers light the way for their teachers, and the students they teach to do the same thing. That it is acceptable to fail is not familiar territory within a system where efficiency and quality control are valued. Insights from educator and author Parker Palmer point to additional challenges involved in taking risks. Palmer suggests that good work is risky business; through experiencing failure, he can recognize the risks. He described that it is easy to become paralyzed by fear. He suggested that once one has known failure, the act of beginning again can be an act of real courage.[40]

> To me, being vulnerable means that you're willing to learn and try things in an area where you're not sure you'll be successful. My assistant principal and I try to model that all the time. We don't have the answers, but we're going to continue to try things. So being vulnerable by being willing to work together and fail forward, and if we don't get it, we're going to learn from it. The worst that will happen is it won't be successful, but something out of that will help us do better next time, or know what not to do the next time.
>
> **- Christine, School Principal**

Overcoming paralysis. Being paralyzed by fear suggests a way to understand the challenge that exists when we invite our adult learners to risk making mistakes and failing as they seek new ways of leading the learning of their students. Joe attempts to lessen the heavy burden of being afraid to fail by making his learning visible to staff. He models his learning process as one that includes struggles.

Openness. Joe describes his openness to be seen as someone who has not got it all figured out. He intentionally models a process for learning to provide his staff with an example to follow. Through his modeling, he makes it evident that if a principal, the leader of a school, is willing to be seen as someone who is an open-to-learning professional, the fertile ground for staff to do the same is being cultivated.

Joe demonstrates the importance of authenticity in the behavior of principals, described by educational researchers Megan Tschannen-Moran and

Christopher R. Gareis as "a willingness to be oneself—to truthfully represent one's beliefs and feelings, as well as owning up to one's foibles."[41] Joe's willingness to ask for input and suggestions from his staff also demonstrates to them he values them as important contributors to the community of learners.

Foot Soldier or Warrior?

Leaders who take this courageous approach to leadership—an approach that requires a shift from being the one with all the answers to the one who also questions, who makes mistakes, and openly shares his or her humanness in the process—moves beyond simply being a foot soldier mindlessly following orders from the top. This leader is a true warrior, battling against a system that no longer serves today's students. This is a leader who suffers the pain associated with being real; a real person with the cracks in their armor exposing vulnerabilities; a real person who questions the way things have always been done, who is driven to find a new way, to test new ideas. This is someone who will endure the reprimands that come from the top when you are too much out of the box or when unrealistic expectations, derived from misunderstood data believed to represent success for all learners, are not being met. It is this brave warrior who must go to battle against parents who understand school only through their own experiences, against teachers reluctant to enter into the same unsafe learning space with their leaders, and against their leaders, those in authority, who are under pressure and scrutiny from their board and the government to produce clear results that can be counted and understood simply. Is this warrior brave to enter onto this uncertain battlefield? Or is this warrior foolish for abandoning the safety and security of the known and familiar?

I try to be very intentional about being transparent in my own learning as well. So, whatever it is that I'm learning about, I'm sharing that out. If there are challenges that I'm struggling with, I'm asking for help from others. I think that's the whole leading by example thing. I think that you can plan really good things, but in the absence of a culture of trust, risk taking, and collaborative opportunities, you can have the best-laid plan in the world, and it doesn't have a lot of impact. But I think if you have culture right, then the opportunities to learn from one another just build on that.

- Joe, School Principal

I, bravely or foolishly, headed onto the battlefield, vulnerable to an attack from the enemy. I was a warrior, not a foot soldier, on this day, Awards Day, at my school. The foot soldier would have followed orders, marched on, picking out the top student with the highest marks to showcase among the student body and selected parents. All obedient foot soldiers do that, right? Follow the rules. Do not disrupt the system.

But I was not a foot soldier. I was a warrior! I was ready for battle. I needed to make a change. We were changing. We were shifting from a traditional junior high with a competitive model of marks-based ranking and sorting of students to a collaborative, growth-oriented community of learners. I had experienced the Awards Day exclusivity as a parent and a teacher where only the chosen ones were invited to the Awards Day Assembly; only the parents of those students who had achieved excellence were on the guest list, while the entire student body of the school attended and watched the same handful of students receive medal after medal after medal. Interesting, I was always happy to attend awards ceremonies as a parent. What parent doesn't want to see their child highlighted for the rest of the school community to see? But my kids did not want to attend. Was it because they didn't care? Was it because the awards ceremonies were boring? Or was it because my kids were not receiving the full array of medals that a few of the others proudly displayed, growing heavier around their necks after each new award was presented.

Many of these bright, keen learners would likely have achieved excellence despite what the teacher did during class time. These learners were among the privileged. Often, they came from families who valued school and supported their children to achieve at high levels (sometimes by even doing the homework assignments for their children!) I was determined to have learning go differently at my school.

My teachers were shifting toward a more collaborative approach to learning where students were encouraged not to compare their achievement to that of their peers. Instead, students were expected to compete against themselves. This had been a four-year journey toward a stronger focus on formative assessment, students co-creating success criteria, making visible their thinking and learning, with ongoing goal setting and students being involved in their own assessment and the assessment of their peers. Students were learning how to speak to their own learning and show their parents evidence of their growth. Today, I was armored up, ready to defend our new approach to Awards Day that aligned more closely with our focus on formative assessment. This meant that recognition would not be given to only the accomplishments of the few. Our celebration of student learning would no longer follow a scarcity model. It was an outdated school ritual that needed to go.

I stood at the doorway, watching the school assembly come to life as our 600+ students entered the gym. Then I saw the parents, the many parents, seated in a section reserved just for them, our special guests who did not need an exclusive invitation to join us on this day. Today, all were welcome. There they sat, some so very proud, smiling, with cameras ready to take pictures of their bright, talented son or daughter being recognized in front of the entire student body for receiving the highest marks in their grade level. Our student master of ceremonies hosted the program, which included student performances and special recognition for the outstanding volunteerism and social responsibility demonstrated by a vast majority of the student body. There were no awards. At the conclusion of the school-wide assembly, parents were invited to exit the gym and join grade-level learning community gatherings for more informal celebrations. These celebrations focused on the abundance of growth of all learners as teachers created ways to highlight the accomplishments, throughout the year, of every student.

How were the parents responding to this change? I waited: heart pounding, nervous, anxious, afraid, pretending to be brave, confident, assured. Surely, I would be confronted, maybe publicly in the gym, for breaking tradition. Was this all a big mistake? An experiment doomed to fail due to the miscalculated readiness of my teachers, the students, and their families?

Existing in this unpredictable, contentious space is what it means to be a leader who nurtures growth. It is more than just talk. It is being willing to act and change processes and structures that no longer serve the shared vision of what it means to be a community that learns. It does not always go well. On this day, it did. We had replaced a worn-out tradition with something far more meaningful to teachers, students, and their families. We were learning a new way to be together.

Experiences like this one led me to a deeper understanding about the fear associated with new learning, growth, and change that involves risk taking. I am becoming more aware of the armor we encase ourselves in to provide safety and protection from the fear of being exposed for the imposters we are. The notion that teachers and leaders are not experts in all matters related to student learning suggests that intentional leadership practices, those that model vulnerability and risk taking, are what is needed if teachers are to become learners themselves. Leaders who nurture the growth of others understand and model the willingness to take risks and open themselves up to making mistakes as they suit up with new armor. This is armor that sees them not as experts, foot soldiers compliantly following the traditions of top-down leadership from the past, but new armor that has cracks and leaves these warriors exposed and vulnerable as co-learners with their teachers, students, and families. By cultivating fertile ground that provides a safe, trusting place to engage in learning, leaders might be in a position to better support the growth of individuals in a school community that learns together.

Honoring Others

We now turn to an additional understanding that emerged for a leader who intends to be together differently with their people and who enters a community that nurtures each other's growth. When leaders show up alongside their teachers to know and understand them as individuals, they can uncover the unique contributions each individual can make and support them in their continued growth. This way of being demonstrates authentic valuing of every member of the community. This idea is presented beautifully in these words of author Douglas Wood:

> Jack pines...are not lumber trees [and they] won't win many beauty contests either. But to me this valiant old tree, solitary on its own rocky point, is as beautiful as a living thing can be....In the calligraphy of its shape against the sky is written strength of character and perseverance, survival of wind, drought, cold, heat, disease....In its silence it speaks of...wholeness...an integrity that comes from being what you are.[42]

The word integrity can be traced back to the fourteenth-century Latin word *integritatem*. It means soundness, wholeness, completeness.[43] Parker Palmer maintains that "the more dividedness we perceive in each other, the less safe and sane we feel."[44] He suggests that when as leaders we align our inner and outer selves, we create a sense of safety and trust among others; we lead from authenticity rather than from a script. Incongruence, he observes, "undermines our morale, relationships and our capacity for good work."[45]

When leading from a place of integrity and wholeness, leaders can help others find meaning and integration in themselves. How do leaders support others to feel valued and whole, to be fully who they are? I was deeply moved by Joe's descriptions of the values that guide his life and work; these are values he shares with his staff at the start of each new school year. It's what he stands for and believes in, and it is something he openly talks about with those he leads at his school:

> Honor...and I talk about that being very close to respect, but for me, honor is like another level to respect that you think about being very intentional. Like, I could go into Starbucks and I could be respectful to the environment without anybody necessarily feeling like I added value to them. So being disrespectful in Starbucks may be causing a scene and making a mess and ruining someone's conversation. Being respectful might be being respectful of your conversation but I'm not really adding any value whereas honor would be that intentionality of "I'm buying a coffee. It's for you because I want to make your day better." And so, I don't think there's really any such thing as a neutral moment in human interaction. It's either adding value or taking value away. Honor would seek to add value and dishonor would take value away.

What struck me about this part of Joe's interview was, first, how transparent and open he is with others. He models the integrity that comes from being what you are. Second, I had never considered the word honor the way Joe described it. Etymological tracings of the word honor reach back to the thirteenth century, derived from the Old French word *honuren*. It means to do honor to, show respect to.[46] Educator, author, and entrepreneur Stephen Covey speaks about showing respect:

> Demonstrate Respect is based on the principles of respect, fairness, kindness, love, civility. The overarching principle, however, is the intrinsic worth of individuals—the importance of each human being as a part of the human family.[47]

As Covey describes it, showing or demonstrating respect is connected to an overarching principle that recognizes the importance and worth of each individual. This is how I understand what Joe is getting at when he speaks about honoring others. He described respecting others as more of a neutral way of being. Honoring, on the other hand, is adding value; it is an elevation of the word respect. His way of being with his school community is to *increase* the value of others.

This is not an easy undertaking. To make time to deeply understand each adult learner requires suspending judgment and refraining from making assumptions. Learners in this kind of community that learns together feel they are valued and they matter to the ongoing growth of the organization. At the same time, they demonstrate an openness to address gaps in their understanding. The walls of defensiveness drop and limited understanding is exposed and addressed because they recognize that all individuals need to continuously adapt and identify areas for growth.

Researcher and author Brene Brown shares her definition of a leader as "anyone who holds her- or himself accountable for finding potential in people and processes."[48] Brown describes how to take a strengths perspective in moving people forward in their learning and growth. When viewing performance from the strengths perspective, the opportunity is offered to examine struggles in the context of capacities, talents, competencies, possibilities, visions, values, and hopes. It requires "us to consider our positive qualities as potential resources."[49]

Austrian neurologist, psychiatrist, and holocaust survivor Victor Frankl wrote about the unconditional value of individuals. He shared that the value of every person stays with him or her, and it does so because it is based on the values he or she has realized in the past. It is not contingent on the usefulness he or she might retain in the present.[50] Parker Palmer contributes to this understanding of the value of individuals and our responsibility as teachers and leaders to work with others so it recognizes their value. He shares the story of the Woodcarver, a Taoist tale from the teachings of fourth-century BCE Chinese master Chuang Tzu. In the story, Khing, a master carver, makes a bell stand of precious wood. Palmer describes how this is akin to relational work that nurtures growth in people:

Khing knows differently. Like every good gardener, potter, teacher, and parent, he understands that the "other" with which we work is never mere raw material to be formed into any shape we choose. Every "other" we work with is its own nature, its own limits and potentials, with which we must learn to co-create if we hope to get real results. Good work is relational, and its outcomes depend on what we are able to evoke from each other.[51]

The relational work of knowing the other with its own nature, limits, and potential requires *being present to the other*. My doctoral research supervisor, Sharon Friesen, shares that presence requires a willingness to "submit…to walk the same landscape over and over again no matter how apparently fruitless or painful the steps, when we just keep showing up without expectation, then grace bestows insight and we uncover ourselves in ways that remain to me utterly mysterious." That is what she modeled for me in the four years of our work together throughout my doctoral program. I suggest it is by showing up, being with others, that we not only uncover ourselves, but we are also there to help others uncover themselves. If we are to work as leaders toward bringing out the potential in those around us, we must know our teachers—know them in the context of their work.

Walking Beside

I remember a conversation I had with one of my principal colleagues about getting into teachers' classrooms. She felt very awkward about just walking in; she believed she needed an invitation and it all just seem so contrived, so formal. I suggested the way in was through the students. Get to know the students, on the playground, talk to them in the hallways, discover what they are learning, get involved with their learning and talk to the teacher about this. Do this more and more. Teachers love to share their students and the learning of their students; they get excited and want to include you in the classroom experiences when it is about the students and not about them. This is what it means to walk beside teachers, to just keep showing up without expectation. This is when grace bestows insight and we uncover our teachers in ways that remain to me utterly mysterious.

The armor that teachers wear to protect themselves from being vulnerable extends to the walls they put up around their classroom spaces to keep others out and protect their work life from judgment. Getting into classrooms often takes a backseat to the numerous managerial expectations of a school leader. If an evaluation report is due, getting into classrooms takes a priority; however, the day-to-day responsibility of being with teachers, engaging in conversations around learning, and the informal opportunities to walk beside teachers in the context of team meetings, classroom instruction, or professional learning experiences appears to be more of a challenge to prioritize in many principals' busy schedules. It almost feels like a cloud of awkwardness or uncertainty hovers over the relationship and day-to-day connection between an experienced teacher and an administrator.

I felt this in my interactions with teachers over the years. It was far easier to spend time in the classrooms of early-career teachers compared with teachers who have extended experience teaching subjects and grade levels in which I had little or no experience. At best, I felt insecure in my ability to offer any feedback that might be valuable to these teachers. In the worst-case scenario, if I engaged in an in-depth conversation with these individuals, I feared I might be exposed for the imposter I sometimes believed I was: a principal without an in-depth knowledge of all grades and subject areas of the curriculum or experience with all developmental levels of students within my school.

I was curious about how other leaders build learning relationships with their teachers. Christine and Reia shared their practice of going into their teachers' classrooms as a way to "walk beside" their adult learners. Research from an Alberta study found that "teachers want more opportunities to engage

I find that it's so much more powerful if I go to them than if I ask them to come to me. There's something about the formality of an office, so going to them and visiting their classroom and just sitting with them for a few minutes or coming...in we weren't always welcome in all classrooms. Everything stopped; "Can I help you?" kind of questions were asked. Whereas now that's not the case. So, having those little touch-base conversations all the time are really important, but to just listen: "Tell me more."

Teachers need to feel heard there's no doubt about that.

- Christine, School Principal

in collaborative conversations about their teaching practice."[52] These opportunities can be created when others come alongside them, in the context of their teaching practice, to develop relationship around the work of teaching and learning, not in formal evaluative roles but in less structured, fluid ways that focus on the learning of students. All three leaders from my study shed light on how they "walk beside" their teachers, opening up dialogue about student learning by being present in different ways than have traditionally been the case. Rather than conversations taking place in the principal's office, these leaders speak about fertile ground for new relationships of learning being cultivated in spaces more closely connected to where teachers carry out their work: in their classrooms.

These leaders in my study described the fertile ground for learning together as being outside of formal office settings. Instead, they connected to the context where teaching and learning happens: within the classrooms and gathering areas of the school. They described how being just part of the fabric of day-to-day life within the school creates an image of the interconnectedness between leader, teacher, and students. For example, Joe shared in a conversation that he stopped setting up shop in his office and, instead, uses a portable desk he wheels into areas of the school at different times. This allows him to respond to whatever's happening in the classroom and then have a conversation around that. This different way of being together breaks down the walls that teachers erect to protect themselves and keep their teaching practice private and the walls that keep principals isolated and separate from the day-to-day life of the school. It is a hopeful sign that fertile ground is being created that will open them up to a new way of being together and learning together.

You have to find the time to be with teachers. If you can't get into your classrooms, if you don't know your kids, if you don't know how to support your staff; then you're not doing your job.

It does mean lots of paperwork and things I do at home, so that I have what I call my "protected time" to get in.

They do see me enough in the classroom. Students don't even look up, which I love. I can't stand when I walk in a room and they say, "Good morning Mrs. ____". They just keep going. I'm just part of the fabric, and they don't get nervous.

- **Reia, School Principal**

Within this informal day-to-day practice of being with each other, teachers and the work they do inside their classrooms can be understood more deeply. Conversations about students and their learning can emerge effortlessly through the practice of simply being together. Within this space, teachers can feel safe to inquire into their practice as Rumi pondered, *"beyond ideas of wrongdoing and rightdoing."*

When a leader creates this safe space to enter into dialogue around student learning—a space that feels free from judgment—authentic, contextual learning can emerge. When a leader notices the strengths of teachers and has built the relational trust to go deeper, ask the next question, help a teacher see for themselves how they might get better, then the fertile ground for a learning organization to take root has been cultivated. The leader who recognizes the unique contributions that others might make to the community of learners, can enact the role of what Brazilian author Paulo Coelho describes as the alchemist. It is by helping others to realize their "Personal Legends" through nurturing their growth and honoring their own unique nature that transformation is possible.[53] Fertile ground is needed for teachers to enter into the work of becoming alchemists for one another. The fertile ground these leaders, as attentive gardeners, are creating requires constant and continuous care and attention:

"You are wise, because you observe everything from a distance," the boy said. "But you don't know about love. If there hadn't been a sixth day, man would not exist; copper would always be just copper and lead just lead. It's true that everything has its Personal Legend, but one day that Personal Legend will be realized.

So, each thing has to transform itself into something better and to acquire a new Personal Legend, until, someday, the Soul of the World becomes one thing only...That's what alchemists do. They show that, when we strive to become better than we are, everything around us becomes better too."

- Paulo Coelho, Author

- Joe speaks to responding to the unpredictability that exists within human dynamics and interactions within a classroom. He honors the uniqueness of each of his adult learners and carefully tends to their needs in a given context at a given moment.
- Reia's voice sheds light on the significance of knowing your people

so you can carry out your first and most important responsibility as a school leader: supporting their growth. Reia observed that she knows of what is happening in every classroom; she may not always know how to react or respond, but she recognizes it is her careful attention to the learning taking place within each classroom that will provide opportunities for her teachers' practices to grow.

- Christine opens up the space for listening to others and taking time to engage in conversations that take place where staff feel rooted and connected to their work: the classroom.

Walking beside teachers, entering into those mysterious places, their isolated classrooms—where you are not always sure what you will uncover—is a responsibility that cannot be put aside in the busy day-to-day life of a school principal. It is far easier to suppress that intuition that addresses you and calls you to enter into the classrooms where more work, more support, more coaching, and more time might be needed. What darkness lurks within? What questionable practices need to be exposed so that *open to learning conversations*[54] can be initiated?

Nurturing growth is not just about working with the keen learners who are open to continuous improvement. This is the challenging work of really being with your class of learners, ALL the teachers. It means walking beside those who do not necessarily welcome your presence or your questions. These are the dark places where openness, growth, and learning are stifled by fear of judgment, fear of exposure, and lack of trust.

Into the Dark

I knew something was not right. She looked exhausted. Last year, she bravely stepped in to take over the teaching assignment of her murdered colleague. She patiently and courageously faced the challenge of showing up, day-in and day-out, for those grieving, devastated students who had lost their cherished teacher. She listened to them, respected them, and honored her colleague's memory by keeping the learning moving forward for the troubled teenagers in her care. She demonstrated commitment, dedication, and strength at a time of intense emotional upheaval.

This year, there were signs she was struggling. I needed to spend more time in her classroom. It was my responsibility to shed some light into the darkness that was disabling growth within that classroom. I remember feeling sick the day I walked into her classroom. What was going on? How can I stop this train wreck before it takes its toll? She knew I was coming to her classroom on this day. She had so carefully and thoughtfully designed an engaging learning task for students, except no one was learning. Student behavior was out of control and she was straining to keep the train from derailing.

I knew I had to come up with a plan that would create the conditions for her and her students to learn. I was burdened with the weight of it all. What if I could not salvage this mess? Whose responsibility is it when a talented, dedicated teacher cannot succeed in her chosen profession, her calling? Is it all on me? Was I to blame for not seeing this sooner? Was it my fault for not ensuring the class lists were more carefully balanced? Did I do this to her by changing her grade level and expecting she learn new curriculum and face the challenge of a very difficult class? These decisions can affect a career. These decisions can influence student learning. This was all so much to be responsible for.

I needed to create conditions for her to thrive. How could I blame this lettuce for not growing? She needed support and it was my responsibility to provide it for her rather than judge her based on an overwhelming number of factors that were stacked up against her. These decisions weigh heavily on the leader's mind; however, the right approach to take is always to create the conditions for growth. I made changes that would see this teacher become successful, starting with adjusting her class list, that changed the interpersonal dynamics of her classroom significantly. I created team teaching opportunities for this teacher so she could be mentored by the school's learning coach. With the adjustments and support, this teacher flourished.

Structures and processes that prevent leaders from making time and providing space for learning to be nurtured among the adult learners are entrenched throughout the system. It is an act of courage to battle against these controlling forces to honor individuals and their growth within the organization. As a specific example: district policy for evaluations of probationary contract teachers must be completed within the first three months of a teacher's employment with a final, career-determining evaluation to follow after only eight months on the job. This creates a challenge for leaders intentional about supporting the growth of early-career teachers.

The practice of teaching is complex. It cannot be expediently and efficiently developed and then evaluated within a three-month window of time. Leaders suffer the extraordinary burden of being held accountable to produce two summative evaluations of these individuals within the first year of their probationary contracts. In my district, probationary contract teachers could not have a second year on a probationary contract; they had to prove themselves within the first year or be cut loose. What a heavy weight this is for principals as they decide about a teacher's career in such a short period, long before they can spend the needed time working with these teachers, supporting their new learning and growth within a very demanding, complex profession.

Sometimes I went to battle to advocate for a longer interval within which to make such important decisions, decisions that would affect not only the career trajectory of the teacher but also have significant effect on hundreds of future students if I made the wrong decision in recommending a teacher for a continuous contract. Being a leader committed to the ideal that everyone can improve and learn is not some starry-eyed optimism that unrealistically believes everyone who enters the teaching profession is meant to stay in the profession. A principal who leads the learning within a school community must recognize when it is time to decide to guide an individual out of the profession, for the students and their learning.

The ambiguous, difficult decisions ultimately rest on the shoulders of the lone warrior, the school principal. It is this individual, alone, who must commit to having challenging conversations, spending valuable time gathering information and evidence of learning to decide if the difficult and heart-wrenching experience of evaluating a veteran teacher is to be undertaken. The teacher's future in the profession rests on decisions that the principal makes; this is the tightrope a brave leader must walk on. There are no guarantees that all will go smoothly. A professional association is armored up and ready to go to battle on behalf of the struggling teacher, a professional association that often neglects their responsibility to support the principal, too. This is the tension lived out by a leader committed to growth for all learners.

Leaders, as master teachers who deeply empathize with and understand the joy and struggle of teaching, might be just the individuals who can provide the fertile ground for their staff to flourish as learners. This idea is echoed in this statement by sociologist Judith Warren Little: "Imagine that you would become a better teacher, just by virtue of being on the staff of a particular school—just from that one fact alone."[55] Leaders, brave warriors and attentive gardeners who walk beside their teachers, enter into those dark spaces where fear and uncertainty live and cultivate relational trust. They nurture staff learning that, in turn, influences student learning; they might be the difference in creating the fertile ground that sees everyone become better.

For Reflection

Chapter Four: A Different Way to Be Together

1. What have you seen or heard among your staff that would lead you to believe there is a high level of trust in your school community?

2. In what ways do you model risk taking and mistake making to your staff?

3. How do you share your values and beliefs with your staff? In what ways do you demonstrate these?

4. In what ways do you increase the value of others within your school community or within your school district?

5. How do you walk beside your teachers? Beside your principals? What impact does this have on their practice? What impact does this have on student learning?

6. How do you decide about hiring, supervising, and evaluating your teachers? Your principals? What would you like to do differently?

7. What policies and practices are in place to provide direction and support for district leaders?

Chapter Five

Feeding Off Each Other

It's been interesting to team teams so we're already thinking about next year: how do we pair people so that people really feed off each other and do amazing things?

- Reia, School Principal

What if we encountered others as contributors to our collective growth?

When Reia made this comment: "People really feed off each other," ...I was hooked! There was something so profound in this simple phrase. It surfaced powerful memories of a time when my teaching colleagues and I were in synchronous flow; we were able to "feed off each other."

What does it mean to become nourished and energized by your colleagues? How do leaders create this way of being together? As a school principal, I observed this collective feeding frenzy erupt among my teachers. When the conditions were created for each to contribute to the collective in a way that mattered for their students, an effortless flow occurred within the team.

Reia's insight about the synergy of teamwork is a reminder to leaders of the need to continually create, cultivate, and steward the relationships required for learning to take root. There is a "field...that grass"; there is fertile ground where souls meet and there is only us, we who are open to a new way to be together. A closer interrogation of the meaning of these words uncovered a new way of understanding the interdependent learning relationships that are possible in the dance of collaboration. It is complex and challenging to establish fertile ground that cultivates team learning. It requires shifting from traditional top-down authority structures that impose orderly control to an authentic approach embedded in day-to-day practical contexts.

Within this team-learning environment, the conditions that allow for the social nature of learning are created. Those involved have ongoing opportunities to process and challenge each other's ideas. The opportunity to feed off each other is

The days of the principal as the lone instructional leader are over.

We no longer believe that one administrator can serve as the instructional leader for an entire school without the substantial participation of other educators.

The old model of formal, one-person leadership leaves the substantial talents of teachers largely untapped.

Improvements achieved under this model are not easily sustainable; when the principal leaves, promising programs often lose momentum and fade away.

**- Linda Lambert,
Educational Researcher**

amplified when individuals, including leaders, can put their power positions aside and enter into genuine, open dialogue with others where compliant agreement is not sought after; rather, differing perspectives, experiences, and insights that contribute to the team's ability to adapt and improve are considered evidence of successful teamwork.

Leaders who attempt to flatten the system's hierarchical structure to create an authentic team-learning environment cannot ever abdicate themselves of the responsibility that comes with the role of school principal. A tightrope exists and it is to be walked upon carefully for there is no safety net below. Step forward, brave warrior; it is about doing what is right, not what is safe.

Nurturing growth, being together differently to feed off each other suggests enacting leadership differently. The principal cannot be the sole individual at the top of the food chain anymore. The complex work of school leadership requires a collective approach drawing on the ideas, talents, and voices of many.[56]

> A community is the mental and spiritual condition of knowing that the place is shared, and that the people who share the place define and limit the possibilities of each other's lives.
>
> It is the knowledge that people have of each other, their concern for each other, their trust in each other, the freedom with which they come and go among themselves.
>
> **- Wendell Berry, Poet**

Rumi reminds us: *The door is round and open.* It is the teachers, working and learning together across corridors, departments, and disciplines who hold the key for collective instructional leadership that will drive educational reform.

What can leaders do to create the fertile ground that nurtures growth and learning among their school staff members, that supports rather than blames? Is it time to let go of the overused and often misunderstood term *professional learning community* to seek a different understanding of what it actually means to be a community that learns together?

How might we define and limit the possibilities of each other's lives through the knowledge we have of each other, in our concern for each other, through our trust in each other?[57] Is it possible to create a shared space, the fertile ground, where there is freedom provided to authentically be who you are, where risks can be taken to explore new and unfamiliar landscapes of learning? What should leaders understand and be able to do to create this "field, that grass" that nurtures growth and provides a different way to be together where people really "feed off each other"?

Live Encounters

Parker Palmer describes live encounters as partnerships in which the full powers of two or more beings are at play. It is through these live encounters with other that the opportunities for seeing one's own thinking in a new light are possible, complex problems can be solved, and shared understanding can be developed through dialogue. An individual learner working in isolation does not achieve what is possible without the contributions of the group.[58]

Collective learning exists in school communities that engage in team learning through dialogue that opens up shared understanding and where there is a collective responsibility to engage in learning that responds and adapts to the complex day-to-day needs of a vibrant, dynamic community of student learners. A collective differs greatly from a collection of individuals and is far more challenging to establish. A collective culture of thinking has qualities that include a sense of purpose to their learning and developing commitment to the task and to the learning of the group. These qualities contribute to creating a sense of community promoting equity where everyone's contributions are valued. Ultimately, this leads to the emergence of a non-hierarchical structure where the leaders are also learners.

Additionally, experiencing challenge is important and learning is enhanced when group members are pushed to do their best. This is a tall order to expect from within busy, demanding school environments comprised of diverse individuals not necessarily seeing their role as a teacher to include collective responsibility for the learning of their colleagues. The principals in my doctoral research discussed how they were attempting to create team-learning environments that were more than just a collection of individuals. Joe observed, "I think that's the dance of collaboration and forming these teams has to be meaningful and relevant to the work of each of those people."

Team-learning networks are needed that are present in higher performing school systems, as it is here we see, says President and founding CEO of *Generation: You Employed* Mona Mourshed and her colleagues, "mechanisms that make teachers responsible to each other as professionals for both their own performance and that of their colleagues."[59] Creating collaborative team-learning networks among staff so they can collectively develop an evidence-based teaching practice focused on meeting student learning needs provides opportunity for people to feed off each other to improve student learning. A high impact on student learning results when staff collaboratively design their professional learning to address the learning needs of students.

The call is made for a new way of organizing schools to highlight a team-oriented model of professional learning that breaks down the walls of isolation. This organizational learning structure involves arranging staff into teams to educate students together to create conditions that allow for the social nature of learning. Those involved have ongoing opportunities to process and challenge each other's ideas.

"Don't you three ever stop talking 'shop.' Relax, enjoy your break, talk about a football game or something." A colleague light-heartedly shared a comment of this nature with my teaching team in the staffroom one noon hour. His teasing tapped into something that reminded me then, and now, of the climate of staffrooms and teacher talk, and the different nature of the talk when there is a culture of a learning community taking root within a school. These conversations are very different.

The talk was rooted in the learning of students. Were the students understanding? What could we do differently to improve on the experience for our students? Who noticed Colin's writing? Did you see the way Diane led her group through that experiment? Why can't Susan work with Kevin? Our professional learning happened day-in and day-out as we continuously inquired into our practice, collectively, to see if our new learning about designing more student-owned, authentic learning was deepening the students' understanding and contributing to their growth.

My colleagues and I teamed up to share teaching space, students, the design of our learning, and our challenges and successes. We no longer felt the isolation of going it alone as teachers. But the experience of working so closely with other adult learners did not lighten our load. It created additional demands on our commitment. The work was time consuming and challenging, but it was energizing! *Let the beauty we love be what we do,* urges Rumi. We engaged in open, honest dialogue about pedagogy, our students' learning needs, and how each of us could move forward in ways not about our individual wants and needs but grounded in the needs of our collective. It was, truly, the most rewarding time of my career as a classroom teacher.

This way of being together in community was a powerful experience that transformed the way I understood collaboration. This way of coming together in a space created for my colleagues and I to engage in problem solving and collective learning within a trusting environment was the fertile ground needed to feed off each other. The school principal created the fertile ground for this to happen. She extended trust to our team to take over the scheduling for students; she provided the team with common planning time to design learning; she provided the resources and set up a professional learning series that introduced the team to a new pedagogical approach; and sat with the team often, engaging in dialogue around our learning as it affected our students' learning.[60]

She understood that evidence of the effect of our learning on students would be found in a wide range of artifacts, demonstrations, and processes, and patiently supported our learning as we explored a new way of being together. I had experienced, first hand as a teacher, a new way to learn with my colleagues made possible by a leader with the vision to change our professional learning structure and practice. I had been awakened to something that had the potential to deepen the learning for students.

Don't go back to sleep, you must ask for what you really want. I knew I wanted to create the fertile ground for this kind of collaboration among teachers I worked with as I grew into my role as a school administrator. I wanted the teachers and other administrators to really feed off each other and do amazing things. I had experienced the life-giving energy of collaboration that transformed my teaching practice; I wanted to bring this gift to all of my teachers in my role as administrator.

Interestingly enough, the rewards that come from collaborating involve a great deal of struggle. Although creating, nurturing, and sustaining the growth of a learning community has been the most challenging work I have engaged in as a school teacher

> Teachers are constrained or enabled in their daily practice by the work of school leaders…effective leaders can build the improvement cultures in which effective educators make sustainable changes in routine professional practices and learn to lift student outcomes.
>
> **- Simon Breakspear, Educational Researcher**

and principal, it has held the most promise. As a principal, I invested time and effort, continuously, trying to bring teachers together into highly effective teams that would draw on each other's strengths, find energy and creativity in the power of the collective, and share the successes and struggles of the complex world of teaching.

Sometimes, I wondered if any of it was worth the trouble, especially when I had individuals approach me, in tears, complaining about the dysfunction on their team. I had to engage in difficult conversations when I could see and hear the dissent among teachers who could not move past mistakes that each other made, or when they could not openly listen to the ideas of others to strengthen their work, or when they would become offended as others offered feedback on the work of their students. We are all so professionally and personally invested in our work. It is understandable that critiques of our practice might feel like a personal attack. However, when a team was in flow, nothing could stop them from feeding off each other.

I was struck by the creative process I had experienced as a school principal trying to design teaching assignments, bring teachers together into teams so they would "honor" the work of each other, add value to the group, and learn together in ways that would create the conditions for powerful, authentic learning for their students. All three leaders who participated in my study spoke to the importance of creating space for teachers to come together, to learn within the context of their day-to-day practice, and to establishing a culture of risk taking firmly embedded in a foundation of trust. No simple recipe is available to follow for how to navigate the complexity inherent in bringing individuals together to create a powerful learning collective. It feels more like a dance.

> I think even trying to move our school to a really collaborative culture, where we learn together and from one another can be an intimidating thing for some people.
>
> **- Joe, School Principal**

The Dance of Collaboration

Joe spoke to this complexity when he used the metaphor "the dance of collaboration." It reminded me of a blog post I wrote several years ago after attending an in-service where the presenter described the role of the teacher as choreographer. This idea struck a chord with me. Principal as choreographer emerged from Joe's comment.

Blog Post: Principal as Choreographer

I am in awe of talented dancers: the movement, the skill, the grace, and strength. Frankly, even though I took several years of dance in my youth (and was very bad!), I have little to no understanding of what is involved as a choreographer. What my limited understanding tells me is that choreographers plan a dance routine and get the dancers to follow their plan. So, how is this any different from the traditional role of a teacher? Plan a lesson and have the students follow your plan (Teacher as "Sage on the Stage"). Then I did a little research [to help me understand more about the role of a choreographer]. I discovered that…the choreographer exposes the dancers to an idea or gives them a challenge, creates a mental picture, and provides them with choices for what to do for themselves. As they explore the creative process, the choreographer observes how the dancers are interacting with the movements and ideas and then decides, in that moment, about how to collaborate with them to change, adjust, and connect to the central idea. The process is fluid, based on taking risks, expressing voice, and communicating ideas. The skilled classroom teacher, as choreographer, follows this same creative, collaborative process. The process is never fixed, always fluid, dynamic, responsive to individuals and allows for individuals to interact with new ideas and understandings so it is meaningful to them. The teacher continuously assists students to connect the smaller pieces to the big, overarching idea to bring coherence and meaning to the process.

Bringing people together, designing the professional learning with teachers is never fixed; it is always fluid, dynamic, responsive to individuals, and allows for individuals to interact with new ideas and understandings so it is meaningful to them. Design begins with knowing the problem space and comes from asking questions: What do students need to learn and be able to do? What should teachers learn and be able to do to create the conditions for learning to occur? What do I as a principal need to learn and be able to do to create the conditions for teachers to learn?[61]

As I became an observer of teachers as my class of learners, noticing the connections between them and the interactions they engaged in through their discussions during team meeting times, I was reminded of my practice as a classroom teacher. I designed learning in my classroom as a teacher to observe how the individuals were interacting with the ideas and then deciding, in that moment, about how to collaborate with them to change, adjust, and connect to the central idea. This requires careful attention and an understanding of the interconnectedness of people who enter into a school building with a common goal: to learn and grow together in service of student learning.

> We laid out the process just as a guide for people to follow. What do my students need? What do I need as a learner? I'm going to engage in the learning process and deepen my understanding and my skills. Whatever they've identified from their students. And then I'm going to design and implement something, and then I'm going to gather evidence. How do I know this is working? And then just live through that process.
>
> **- Joe, School Principal**

Author Melody Beattie, in her book *Journey to the Heart*, discusses her understanding of interconnectedness that emerged when she traveled to the Chaco Canyon in New Mexico. Here, she found remnants of the Anasazi culture. It was through the structures, still in place, that she perceived the subtle effect that each person and each movement in the universe has on all the others. Symbols of interconnectedness were evident in a dwelling where over eight hundred rooms were built in a connected circle. Each room touched the next, and the structure contained all the areas the people needed to work, to live, to play, and to worship. This structure reminded me of the unique design of my middle school. Large open spaces, called pods, were placed in the center of each wing of the school. These common gathering areas were encircled by interconnected classrooms.

Beattie describes the spiritual philosophy of the Pueblo people, descendants of the Anasazi. They live at the center of their universe, understanding that all things are interconnected. All are part of the whole. The boundaries for all things to live are where the sky and the earth touch. The essence of life is shared by all things through cycles of birth and death.

The Pueblo philosophy symbolizes the way we are connected to each other today. Beattie reminds us we are each part of a dance of the universe and that, even if we live alone, we are part of a larger family. Even if we work alone, we are part of an interconnected team. Beattie suggests that we:

Take time to honor your connections, and the impact of each person you've met. See how people have helped shape you; see how you've touched and shaped them. Each interaction creates a ripple affect; each encounter helps shape destiny.[62]

These words reminded me of the heavy responsibility we have when working and learning with others: *each interaction creates a ripple affect; each encounter helps shape destiny.*

* * *

Another funeral for another teacher...again, being asked to speak at *her* funeral; again, listening to the students who wanted a school assembly to celebrate *her* life; again, being brave, putting on the armor. Absolutely no cracks could appear: no tears, no emotion that might signal weakness when I needed to show strength.

I ran into a teacher who used to work at my school. The teacher worked with *her*, before *she* got sick, before I was supervising *her* to help her improve *her* practice, before any of us knew *she* was dying. The teacher I ran into told me about a conversation with *her*, before *she* died. The teacher told me *she* talked about what an honor it was to be on my staff, to have a leader set such high expectations for the teachers. My heart was broken...again. This is the burden of being a leader and walking beside the teachers: each encounter helps shape destiny. I stumbled across a note *she* gave me when we attended the first funeral together:

I have been thinking of you this past week, wondering how you are doing and sending strength your way. I know that when you signed up for this role, that you never thought you would have to lead us through something like this…thank you for leading us toward the light and out of the darkness that encompasses us now.

I had no idea that I would be at *her* funeral only two years later…after meeting with *her*, walking beside *her*, setting expectations for *her* practice. How could I have known *she* was dying? I needed to do what was right for the children in *her* care. I was an attentive gardener, trying to create the conditions for *her* growth. I assigned *her* to work among an effective, dedicated team of teachers so *she* could learn from *her* colleagues. Don't go back to sleep; pay attention to what is happening in this classroom. Was this teamwork creating dependency? Were the children in her class being taught well? Were teachers creating the conditions for ALL students to succeed? How were you helping ALL the teachers learn and get better? How did you activate the teachers to be learning resources for one another? How were you making sure they are ALL contributing to the work? What did I need to know and be able to do to choreograph this dance of team learning?

I think the principal's role is about being a learner alongside the teachers and fostering connections. Sometimes it's just about connecting them to another teacher who's already doing work like this and then supporting that with resources, time, and money. Sometimes, it means creating those conditions, creating those opportunities for them to learn through that. And so then, that creates a really safe place for teachers to begin to be owners of their own learning.

- Joe, School Principal

Joe had something to say on this matter. He saw his role as a learner with his teachers and also surfaced aspects of being a connector among his staff: fluidly and dynamically choreographing their encounters with each other and what it means to create conditions under which a teacher might learn. Live encounters with other have the potential for people to really feed off each other and do amazing things.

Similarly, Reia's staff engages in live encounters through conversations about learning. Reia describes her vision for collaboration where all voices are heard, all voices are valued. This is a different way of coming together than many may have experienced previously through collaboration.

For her part, Christine describes a past experience of collaboration based on a shared understanding—one that many still hold onto—that prevents them from harvesting the real potential coming together into community can provide: the commonly-held belief that collaboration is about creating efficient use of resources to speed up planning processes. With this, Christine opens up an important space for deeper understanding. Valuing efficiency permeates most school cultures; it is a reminder of the strong hold that Taylor's efficiency movement maintains on business and educational institutions.

Rich deep discussion around learning needs to be done in a collective group where all voices are heard, all voices are valued; so that we as professionals heighten the learning. You can't do that in isolation with delegated tasks, but it's a journey, and we have teams all over the map with it.

- Reia, School Principal

Stifled by this looming legacy of tight control and fragmentation of tasks to promote timely, standardized completion, it is understandable that teachers tend to see time spent together is valuable if it creates ways to make the growing complexity of their role more efficient. I saw it often. Teachers equated collaboration time with parceling-out tasks such as sharing photocopied lesson plans. They establish efficient ways to divide the labor, severing interconnected subject disciplines by appointing subject specialists who looked after the creation of an isolated unit of study to pass out to colleagues.

The kind of space that Reia and Christine are exploring for teachers requires a slowing down so, through dialogue, individuals can understand differently. Those who work with us help us to see ourselves differently. They make schools public spaces where teachers have opportunities to observe other teachers and provide feedback, rather than places where teachers are left alone to try and then individually reflect on their practices. Through the assistance of others, one can learn what they cannot see for themselves. As Joe observes, "I think that even at the formative stage, we want to

And you know, back in the day when I started teaching, your idea of collaboration was well here's my lesson plans. Can I have yours? Or here's some photocopies, can I have yours? We rarely ever sat down and had philosophical conversations. It was hallway conversations, right. So I would imagine that's the experience of some of the teachers up to this point as well.

- Christine, School Principal

be supportive and, in this case, I think the person is a learner and wants to grow and just doesn't know how. Maybe he hasn't seen something different."

Entering into dialogue with others within our teaching contexts helps us to see something different. It helps us recognize our own potential from within and provides us with the insight to understand aspects of ourselves that may have gone unnoticed. In dialogue with others, we can see our blinds spots and uncover the future that already exists inside us: As Rainier Maria Rilke tells us, "The future enters into us, in order to transform itself in us, long before it happens."[63]

Physicist and systems theorist Fritjof Capra notes "The uniqueness of being human lies in our ability to continually weave the linguistic network in which we are embedded."[64] In other words, we bring forth a world with others through language. Captra tells us this extends the dance beyond a leader's role of choreographing a team to create a dance of collaboration that exists within our conversations:

We're constantly learning from one another. As a teacher, if I have the trust of my colleagues, and I trust them, I can say, "I'm struggling with this. Help me." And vice versa. And if I have the perspective that this isn't just my class, all of the kids in our school are all of our kids then I think that starts to create a place we start to learn from one another.

I think the second that a teacher experiences the power of, "my job just got easier, and better, and more engaging, and the kids' learning got better, and they're more engaged and have less behavior, and I have less challenges because they're super pumped" and that came from the fact that I wasn't doing this on my own, but it came from one of my colleagues through the process of collaboration.

- Joe, School Principal

In a human conversation our inner world of concepts and ideas, our emotions, and our body movements become tightly lined in a complex choreography of behavioral coordination. Film analyses have shown that every conversation involves a subtle and largely unconscious dance in which the detailed sequence of speech patterns is precisely synchronized not only with minute movements of the speaker's body, but also with corresponding movements of the listener. Both partners are locked into the precisely synchronized sequence of rhythmic movements, and the linguistic coordination of their mutually triggered gestures lasts as long as they remain involved in their conversation.[65]

This dance of conversation—where there is a synchronicity, an energy flow among a collective, where people really feed off each other—is described by Redfield:

> In a truly functional group…the idea is for every member's energy and vibration to increase because of the energy sent by all of the others. When this occurs, everyone's individual energy field merges with everyone else's and makes one pool of energy. It is as if the group is just one body. Sometimes another talks. But in a group functioning this way, each individual knows when to speak and what to say because he truly sees life more clearly.[66]

Creating time and space for thinking are important conditions needed to realize the benefits of a collaborative culture of learning. Members of a collaborative learning organization need to slow down, take time to ask questions, and know the learning, the challenges to learning, and the complex contextual variables that build shared understanding and meaning with a group. After years of asking thousands of people including teachers, administrators, parents, business people, academics, and others, educational researcher Ron Ritchhart compiled a shortlist of what people identified as the qualities of effective cultures of thinking. Included in his list are:

- Everyone's input was valued, creating a sense of respect.
- There was a constant questioning and probing of ideas by everyone in the group, not just the leader.
- The leader was engaged, interested, and passionate. She was a learner with us.
- There was open communication and active listening going on. You felt heard.
- We had time to think, respond, and develop ideas.
- We felt safe to take risks and make mistakes. It was even expected as part of the process.

- There were stimulating group interactions. We liked each other. We pushed and supported one another.
- Our learning was connected to our lives. It had value and meaning.[67]

Christine, Joe, and Reia describe how they prioritize time in their scheduling for teachers to enter into dialogue with each other; learners need time together to feed off each other. The school principals speak of specific work teachers do in the school community to design, plan, learn, and look at evidence of learning. They speak also about creating time, space, and resources for collective learning or for working together on a project based on what teachers felt would enhance their practice. These intentional, pre-planned professional learning opportunities differ from live encounters that emerged more organically based on a pressing need or situation, typically from struggles with students or something that addressed them within the day-to-day practice. The emergent situations were seen as ways to engage in authentic contextual learning with colleagues.

When teachers have the trust of colleagues, they can share their challenges and ask each other for help. Problems to be solved and struggles to be understood provide the authentic opportunities for live encounters that nurture the growth of a community that learns together. Opportunities to nourish each other are available through live encounters that nurture the growth of a school community that learns together. These encounters contribute to building a sense of community. When experienced from the students' perspective, this involves creating a community in which students are routinely engaged in work that contributes to the advancement of ideas beyond their own. It becomes a community in which students are invited to work on real problems or issues through pedagogies requiring them to build on each other's ideas and use authoritative sources as well

But what it's done, is it's created a culture of reflection and learning, and so the teacher will come and say, "I'm really struggling with this kid," and if they haven't come necessarily as prepared as we'd like them to, to those meetings, then we'll support them where they're at, then model for them. It's those discussions that happen during those structures which is those two blocks per week, and they're typically full, and they're full because people are obviously finding them helpful.

- Reia, School Principal

as other information sources as data for their own knowledge building and idea improvement. They ask clarifying questions, creating a rich environment for ideas to evolve into new and more refined forms, and take responsibility for advancing the entire group toward achieving its goal.[68]

Joe's comments about authentic learning for teachers draw on similar principles. From the teachers' perspective, what is required is an understanding and enacting of pedagogies that create the conditions for collective knowledge advancement: learning at the individual and the collective levels. As leaders enact leadership strategies based on the pedagogies that advance learning at the individual and collective levels, they invite teachers to see problems they encounter with creating conditions for learning for individual students as opportunities to engage in the work of problem solving and idea improvement. For example, Reia describes the way her staff is working with each other to bring problems forward with others to break down the walls of isolation so that together—individually and collectively—they can learn from one another.

The Promise of Struggle

Holding onto familiar ways of doing things, staying fixed within ineffective routines and clinging to rigid structures keeps teachers and leaders from opening up to new possibilities that exist when they come together through the real work they do together. Holding onto the familiar, the taken-for-granted, reinforces the fragmentation so prevalent in schools: fragmented curriculum, time, activities, and fragmented lives. Capra described the Buddhist philosophy of suffering that arises when we

cling to fixed forms and categories created by the mind instead of accepting the impermanent and transitory nature of all things. Out of ignorance (avidya), we divide the perceived world into separate objects that we see as firm and permanent, but which are really transient and ever-changing.[69]

The tendency to hold onto rigid categories is a barrier to achieving the potential that exists in human suffering. It prevents us from realizing the fluidity of life and, instead, makes our experience one of "frustration after frustration."[70] People who come together for conversation or dialogue can learn the reason for their coming together was in a need to release their capacities and come to find their own words. Through this process they can see the world as problematic and

> I strongly believe that school is a collaborative place. I've always believed that we need to open our doors up.
>
> **- Christine, School Principal**

in need of change. Viewing the world through a lens of suffering, struggles, and problems provides opportunities to enter into dialogue with others, Greene reminds us, to "engage in the acts of thinking, and...[and] try to transform the world."[71]

Creating fertile ground for a school community that learns together is a key responsibility of the school leader, gardener, warrior, choreographer, and designer of the dance of collaboration. Fertile ground, established through relational trust modeled and nurtured by school principals, where mistakes are viewed as opportunities for new learning, where learners feel safe to expose their vulnerabilities, and where everyone feels valued for their contributions may be places where struggles are welcomed as signals to awaken to new possibilities to know better, do better, and be better. Greene describes this as a breaking free and "breaking through the structures of their world and creating something new."[72] This is only possible, she explains, when "individuals come together in a particular way, when they are authentically present to one another (without masks, pretenses, badges of office), when they have a project they can mutually pursue."[73] This is the fertile ground needed for creating connections between people.

Opening doors and breaking down walls that isolate us from each other create live encounters within a community of wholeness where individuals can feed off each other to pursue learning together and feel authentically connected to each other, their students, and the entire school community. *The door is round and open. Do not go back to sleep.*

A new way of being together, where people feed off each other, is not without conflict, misunderstandings, and tensions. The leader must ensure that every teacher is meeting the expectations for quality teaching as interpreted throughout the day-to-day practice within a dynamic, complex school context. The leader is in the precarious position of empowering the teaching teams to engage in challenging dialogue in the pursuit of designing powerful, authentic learning for students while keeping a close eye and ear on the interactions and evidence of student learning; simultaneously, they are deciding about how and when to intervene when individuals are heading in a direction not aligned with the school's vision for student learning. This is

We are expecting them to open their classroom doors and be willing to observe in their colleague's classroom to improve student learning.

- Reia, School Principal

when the work gets challenging as it is necessary to make needed corrections while also ensuring this is done with the upmost regard for each individual's dignity, professional knowledge, and skills.

When individual teacher practice becomes a collective, collaborative enterprise, the stakes are even higher for ensuring corrective conversations and guided supervision of individual teachers is handled respectfully, thoughtfully, and carefully. While a team approach to learning is ideal, it is still the responsibility of the principal to initiate necessary individual learning and growth conversations. I experienced the difficult moments when changes to individual teaching practice were called for; these situations needed to be addressed behind the closed door of my office. I also experienced the reactive, defensive stance of teachers who misinterpreted the conversation as an attack on their teaching skill and when this led to complaints to our professional teaching association about my leadership. These moments of tension, where feelings get hurt and trust is damaged, are blocks to creating an open, collaborative culture of learning. During these times of struggle, the leader is alone within the school community that learns.

The risk of destroying the trust and cohesiveness among the learning community must be taken, however, to move closer toward the goal of creating the conditions so all learners will succeed. Bouncing back from these challenging times is difficult and trusting that the right decision has been made and the right conversation was had are heavy burdens that weigh upon the sole leader; however, when time has been taken to engage in understanding the contexts, the challenges, and then to provide ongoing support to correct a situation in the spirit of continuous learning and improvement, each conflict and struggle takes the learning relationship to the next level of trust. My experience has been that professionals respond well to conversations that are not about assumptions or blame but entered into with the genuine intention to uncover thinking and promote growth. They see that their leader is investing time in their growth.

Creating fertile ground that nurtures, supports, and sustains a school community that learns together is the responsibility of the principal as lead learner and leader of learners. Fertile ground that nurtures growth requires leaders to recognize that all learning involves risks. For teachers to open up to new learning, a culture of trust must be cultivated. Fertile ground provides a different way to be together: out beyond ideas of wrongdoing and rightdoing, there is a field; I'll meet you there.

Principals who are present walk beside their teachers without judgment, seeking to understand their individual and collective knowledge, skills, and values within the complex contexts of their work to guide, support, listen, and respond, create the conditions that nurture growth as they demonstrate a strengths-based orientation to learning. Leaders who create fertile ground provide opportunities for all learners to contribute in meaningful ways to the collective; they are recognized, valued, and honored. It is within this fertile ground that teachers may then open up to opportunities to feed off each other.

Removing structures and processes that isolate teachers creates the space and time for them to contribute to the advancement of ideas beyond their own. When teachers approach each other, bringing with them their differing experiences and perspectives, the space for collaboration is not experienced as a battlefield—my way versus your way. Instead, it is what Rumi described as grass, that field where we meet together to be together differently. This is a shared responsibility for advancing the entire group toward achieving its goal; it supports the notion that problems or challenges encountered by the group within the day-to-day practice of their work are opportunities to build collective strength, resilience, and creativity in overcoming these obstacles together. Awakening to this different way of being together offers the potential for continual renewal in a school community that learns together.

For Reflection

Chapter Five: Feeding off Each Other

1. What conditions have you created for a team learning environment to flourish in your school community? In your school district?

2. Does your staff have a shared understanding of what a community that learns together is about?

3. What have you noticed about the way colleagues interact with each other, in the hallways? During staff meetings? During team meetings? In the staff room? Is there a culture of collective learning taking root? How do you know?

4. How much ownership does your staff take of their own learning? How do they decide what they need to learn more about? How do you know it is making a difference to student learning?

5. How do you address conflict or problems among teaching teams?

6. How do you know if teams are actually engaged in learning that affects student learning as opposed to meeting to share tasks?

7. Have you seen evidence of the influence teachers are having with each other's learning? What did you notice?

Part Three

—

Renewal

Lift up your hearts.

Each new hour holds new chances
for new beginnings.

Do not be wedded forever
to fear, yoked eternally
to brutishness.
The horizon leans forward,
offering you space to place new steps of change.
Here, on the pulse of this fine day
you may have the courage
to look up and out upon me,
the rock, the river, the tree, your country.

No less to Midas than the mendicant.

No less to you now than the mastodon then.

Here on the pulse of this new day
you may have the grace to look up and out
and into your sister's eyes,
into your brother's face, your country
and say simply
very simply
with hope
good morning.

-Maya Angelou, On the Pulse of Morning

How does a school community engage in continuous learning that is adaptive to a complex, constantly changing context?

It seems to me that the only thing constant in life is change. The New Zealand Koru symbolizes the essence of change in a silver fern frond's life: a cycle of birth, growth, death, and new beginnings. The gradual unfurling of the tightly coiled fern frond represents the life cycle of the fern. This cycle is critical to the well-being of this living organism. We are not that different from the fern.

Cycles of change, like those that exist in the natural environment, occur as a process of constant rejuvenation. The cycle exists as a healthy, natural way to take from the past what is still necessary and relevant, while letting some things die to make space for new growth. This regenerates a system. This natural renewal process is evident in the organizational cycles that occur within a school year. For me, the mystery was to uncover how this renewal process might come to life within a school in a different way: a way that might shift the nature of continuous improvement from being a controlled, mandated expectation directed by the school leader—bound within the fixed schedule of a school year—toward becoming a more fluid process that lives beyond the presence of a leader. Perhaps this will provide insight for how school renewal lives, as a natural process, within every individual.

Cycles of renewal spoken about by the leaders I interviewed revealed deeper understanding of the value of being able to live the questions now instead of expecting to have answers—the truth—pre-determined within a fixed, secure, and closed guideline, standard, or fragmented curriculum outcome. None of this comes without challenge, ambiguity, and a call for assurance that leaders are not experimenting in ways that might be detrimental to the aspirations parents and public have for our youth. It is a contentious position for leaders to be in: understanding the need to break free from the dead wood of a past that does not let them reinvent the new while providing assurance that student learning will not be in jeopardy as they test the waters of change.

As I deepened my understanding of this topic of renewal, I contemplated the message revealed in the poem "On the Pulse of Morning" by Maya Angelou. It spoke to me of an invitation to fearlessly create space for change; from this space, it might be possible for hope to emerge from the wholeness created through community with others. It is the promise of hope from within this poem that lights the way for an exploration of renewal.

Chapter Six

—

Networks of Influence

That constant improvement, feedback cycle, that process…I think the only way that that lives beyond an individual is when it lives in every individual.

- Joe, School Principal

How can we apply concepts from nature to renew our classrooms and schools?

The flow of life in a school has a natural rhythm. The cycles and seasons of a school year reflect those found in nature. Nature's cycle of growth comes into its fullest expression in the summer before gradually winding down in the fall, a time for release of old growth, as it prepares for rejuvenation during the winter months before spring bursts forth. Its arrival signals a rebirth teeming with new growth and the budding promise for new beginnings.

Although similar, the school's cycle follows a slightly different time frame. The process of renewal typically gets underway after the summer months as the excitement and energy that mark the beginning of a new school year build up. Principals are often first to arrive on the scene, ensuring that staffing is set, schedules are ready, and specially requested meetings with new students and families get underway. Teachers come and go with their fresh ideas for the new school year. They often blast into the building, a whirlwind of frenetic activity as they set up furniture and bring in new treasures in preparation for the upcoming year.

As a principal, I engaged in an annual ritual of spending time in the quiet, empty school late in the evening after the staff was long gone before opening our doors to a new school year the next morning. I walked slowly in and out of each classroom, taking time to notice and appreciate the careful attention to every detail representing long hours devoted to preparing for our students. The school was spotless, floors were shiny, walls washed, everything in its place, classrooms painstakingly organized with class lists posted, welcome messages on doors, and the day's schedule mapped out on whiteboards.

I closed my eyes, breathed in deeply, letting the stillness sweep over me as I imagined the energy and excitement that would soon transform these classrooms and hallways the following morning when everyone, staff, students, and families, arrived to begin anew. No other day during the year is like the first day of school. *Here, on the pulse of this fine day*, is the creation of space wherein to place *new steps of change*. Renewal begins.

New Understandings: Innovation or Renewal?

The word renewal is not nearly as common as the word innovation as it relates to the field of education. A closer look at these two terms will help to surface their connection to the concepts uncovered in this next section. The word renewal is derived from a combination of its root words: *re-* meaning "back to the original place; again, anew, once more," also with a sense of "undoing," and *new*—meaning "new, fresh, recent, novel, unheard-of, different from the old; untried, inexperienced." It is interesting that the original meaning for the word *innovate* is to "introduce as new" and, from the Latin innovatus, "to renew, restore;" also "to change." Its intransitive meaning is "bring in new things, alter established practices."[74] Innovation is a term that is on the verge of being overused, resulting in a lack of a common, shared understanding. While the word renewal conjures up images of ecological growth, the word innovate is generally associated with technical growth.

Educational researcher and statistician Andreas Schleicher helpfully clarifies the meaning of innovation that supports the discussion in this chapter:

> Innovation in education is not just a matter of putting more technology into more classrooms; it is about changing approaches so that students acquire the skills they need to thrive in competitive global economies.[75]

Innovations being widely investigated are the nature of learning, learners, educators, and pedagogy, content, and resources. Specifically, innovative practices that disrupt the traditional model of school systems include "the regrouping of teachers, regrouping of learners, rescheduling learning, and changing pedagogical approaches—and the mix of those approaches—to provide better teaching for better learning."[76]

In this chapter, renewal refers to a formative process of continuous growth that addresses the nature of student learning and the way teachers work and learn to engage as adaptive experts. This way of thinking about renewal supports the process of educators working formatively, as noted by the Organization for Economic Co-operation and Development (OECD), "not just with the learners but in terms of the organisational strategies of design and development using rich evaluative information on the teaching and learning taking place."[77] Within this context for renewal, Dutch education researcher Inges Bakkenes and her colleagues posit that teachers

> have to develop another vision on learning and teaching, be motivated to learn about the new pedagogy, understand what the innovation is good for, develop skills to bring the innovation into practice, reflect on their experiments with the new pedagogy in order to learn, and form part of a community of teachers who all are learning new things.[78]

Within a school context, renewal processes seek to engage educators, learners, their families, and the community in collaborative inquiry that will transform schools into more innovative learning environments. A renewal process creating the conditions in schools and learning settings where curiosity is encouraged, developed, and sustained is essential. Curiosity opens up thinking, changes practice, and creates dramatically more innovative approaches to learning and teaching.[79]

Renewal, innovation, and new growth are at the heart of a school community that learns together. This life-sustaining, vital process is not necessarily a daily practice evident in many schools. However, the conversations with the principals who participated in my study revealed their attempts to live out new beginnings and rejuvenation within each of their school communities. Joe shares his understanding of the word innovation in the context of a school community that learns together:

> The word 'innovation' is…funny. Different people define innovation in different ways. So, what may be innovative to me because I never experienced it, may not be that innovative to you. And so, I think in the context of education, it's not about every single teacher completing something that's never been done before. But I think it's about how do we embrace new practice or new ideas or new technology, or innovative ideas that reflect what's happening in the world today? That is the idea of taking risks and not being comfortable with where we're at.

"How do we embrace new practice or new ideas or new technology, or innovative ideas that reflect what's happening in the world today?" While Joe began our conversation on innovation within schools by reflecting on how individual teachers might make sense of that term, he transitions from the actions of a single teacher to reorient the idea of innovation to communal action. This reveals the importance of cultivating dialogical communities where different opinions are considered and decisions result from communal deliberation. In other words, the concepts of renewal and innovation, when lived out in the particular day-to-day life of these school communities, need to be worked out among those within the particular school context. That is what this chapter will attempt to do, by looking at universals from broader research and turning it over within the particular experiences of my colleagues, leaders creating schools that learn together.

New Beginnings

When oriented toward communal action, a school community open to the new creates openings and has established fertile ground to learn together, might embrace processes of renewal that can be understood differently by turning toward ecology to inform their endeavors. These renewal processes seem naturally connected to the beginning of each new school year; however, after reflecting on a remembered conversation with students, I am reminded of something more to be uncovered. I listened compassionately as a group of distressed, upset teenagers shared treasured memories of their teacher shortly after they had learned of her death. Their conversation centered around what made *her* so special to each of them and what they wanted to hold onto, something from *her* that would live on in each. One student talked about a memory that resonated so deeply with me I included it in the eulogy I was asked to give at *her* funeral. The words are with me still:

She always treated every day as a new beginning.

Each new hour holds new opportunities for new beginnings. This is a powerful way of being within a school community. Approached as a new beginning, the space for renewal is created. It points toward not a particular action, but a disposition that might be considered central to individuals committed to renewal. The conversation with these students revealed their appreciation for a teacher open to seeing them with fresh, new eyes each day, following what may have been a situation embroiled in conflict and frustration on the previous day. This memory resonated with me as I sought to understand the conversations with the principals I interviewed.

Renewal, in this sense, is what I have come to understand as a way to sustain growth, freshness, and an openness to continuous learning despite the tendency to close off, put up walls, and make judgments when people or situations create disappointment or become challenging. Students described a teacher who never closed herself off to her students. Instead, she chose to remain open, curious, and connected with her students as each new day opened up: offering space to place new steps of change, free from the weight of past mistakes, dead wood, old wounds.

Every teacher starting a new year in September knows something about this ability to see with fresh eyes, an ability that weaves together remembering and forgetting, taking hold and letting go and sometimes repeating as for the first time.

- David Jardine,
Educational Researcher

This belief in the life-giving power of renewal that comes from new beginnings is one I aimed to live out in the day-to-day practice of leading a school community that learns. Every year, month, day, and hour were an opportunity to open up to growth as it exists in the cycle of nature: a release of the old that no longer serves the needs of the students, to make way for the new. How might I, with my staff, embrace new practice, or new ideas, or new technology, or innovative ideas that reflect what is happening in the world today? This question is one that continuously challenged my school community. A fine balance, an equilibrium needs to be struck between exploring, adapting, and changing based on what our school, classrooms, and students need, while not being so untethered it feels like there is no solid ground to stand on and no safe, predictable routines or structures in place.

For the most part, my school community recognized that it would adapt to what the professionals felt and what research recommended was best for students. I needed to nurture the growth of a critically reflective team encouraged to question old traditions and routines if it was felt they no longer met the needs of students. Renewal was a necessary process that deserved ongoing attention to breathe new life into places where learning was not engaging and students were neither curious nor involved in meaningful work.

I recall an event that happened early in the season of a new school year. Many staff members were expressing frustration about their inability to meet the diverse learning needs of their students. They felt the timetable was too fragmented; they weren't able to spend enough quality time with students, particularly the students who needed more intensive support. The administrative team, of which I was the principal, had adapted the way we were set up that year by restructuring the school timetable, re-organizing groups of teachers for instruction, and putting a new process in place. It was a major overhaul partway through the year but, for this year, for these students, as a collective, my staff felt it was necessary. The school staff adapted, reflected, and I sought advice from researchers. I did not agree to make the same adjustment the following year although there had been a lot of positive feedback from students and parents. Some recognized that, as professionals, our attempt to de-fragment the timetable saw us fragment the classroom communities. The team had over-compensated to solve one problem and, unintentionally, created another problem.

It was through taking risks to explore the new and innovate that my staff team learned, adjusted, and adapted. That was the story of my school, as I remember it: collective problem solving, trying out new solutions, and looking for evidence that what we were doing would be best for our students. Joe, too, spoke of renewal as taking risks and not being comfortable with where we are.

I tried to establish a culture of openness: space that encouraged trying something different or new if the team felt it would lead to better learning for students. This approach was difficult to navigate. I, along with my staff, had to ask hard questions, be willing to discuss changes with our students and our parents, and trust each other along the way. This way of being together reflected a growth-oriented, more organic approach to leading within a school. An orientation of renewal breaks with the mechanistic prescriptiveness lived out in many schools: imposed, regimented routines; linear boxes; and schedules that symbolize outdated, industrialized, mandated approaches.

These two differing paradigms, the mechanistic, structured system and an organic approach for determining how schools might operate, seem to serve dual purposes. On the one hand, the legacy of an industrialized model with regimented routines and structures was put in place to ensure the efficiency and completion of pre-determined achievements of the school system. This mechanistic approach to schooling, highly influenced by Taylor's industrialized business management model, still infuses our schools. The current educational system still holds onto many of the structures handed down from the past: placing value on measurement and the timely, compliant completion of tasks. In the era of industrialized learning models, there was a strong belief that students would do best when given a specific task within a short period of time.

One of the lasting legacies from this model is a bell system that keeps the highly fragmented school timetable in place. The outdated school structures that view students as passive, heeding the cattle call, moving from class to class, teacher to teacher, isolated subject to isolated subject, have mostly remained a permanent fixture at the center of school organizational procedures, even in some of the most so-called innovative schools.

For example, this fragmented, mechanistic school organizational structure permeates the mandated Alberta curriculum. Separated by subjects and grades with prescribed topics, learning outcomes, and times, little room is left for the living: students, teachers, and topics fully alive in the world. Teachers have little to no opportunity to connect ideas or subjects, or connect with the living aspects of the disciplines or topics as they live in the world.

These mechanistic structures isolate and fragment teachers as well. Most of the time, teachers practice in private. Therefore, when invited to work together to learn from and with each other in their school communities, many are at a loss for not only how to engage with each other, but also fail to understand the need for such an undertaking. Many teachers experience such attempts at collaborative endeavors as one more thing to do: an addition to an already busy day. What educators have inherited from Taylor's business management model is a system that rewards a competitive, independent, and efficient individual who can provide the right answers to pre-determined questions to get ahead of the pack. In this way, teachers, learners, and the subject disciplines all have been reduced to fit the institutional machine of schooling.

In contrast, the OECD describes a different design for learning environments that would better reflect an organic, ecological metaphor for school systems. A call for innovating the fundamentals of schooling was made, expressing the need for radically changing core habits and practices that reflect predictability and control. The OECD suggested these learning principles as reflective of growth, interconnectedness, and renewal to guide development of the new structure for the organization of today's learning environments:[80]

Learning Principles	
One	Make learning central, encourage engagement, and be where learners come to understand themselves as learners.
Two	Ensure that learning is social and often collaborative.
Three	Be highly attuned to learners' motivations and the importance of emotions.
Four	Be acutely sensitive to individual differences including prior knowledge.
Five	Be demanding for each learner but without excessive overload.
Six	Use assessments consistent with the aims, with strong emphasis on formative feedback.
Seven	Promote horizontal connectedness across learning activities, and subjects, in-and out-of-school.

Clearly, the call is being made for a renewal of the educational system. The focus is on the creation of vibrant learning communities with spaces for new ways of thinking and boundless opportunities for exploration. Rather than mindless compliance to the disconnected deadwood of old habits and routines of an irrelevant model, interconnected webs of living relationships are created within this structure.

As a school principal who wished to create a school community that learns, I challenged my staff to co-create a culture where we engaged in renewal processes that saw us as an evolving, adaptive, and changing organization, responsive to the changing needs of our students and the complexity of our classrooms. This required never becoming complacent, never going back to sleep, nor becoming rutted in the routines and structures of comfort. Instead, we established fertile ground for new ideas to emerge, for welcoming questions. We re-thought how we looked at curriculum, our classroom configurations, teaching teams, and the design of learning. We looked for ways to stretch leadership among many.

Jardine reminds us that "The human story cannot go on without renewal and regeneration." [81] To deepen understanding of the importance of a renewal process in the life of a school community that learns together, Jardine describes renewal as an orientation and openness to the future that "keeps open the precious possibility to dwell with a boundless heart."[82] Renewal is not creating something new or novel from scratch, with all histories and learning that has come before severed. Instead, renewal is a process of "furtherance." [83] To Jardine, furtherance exists in relation to interpretive work, seeking to rejuvenate and enliven relationships between the young and the old. It allows the new to emerge while enabling the old and already established to regenerate and renew itself to find its life again. It is a process of awakening "deadened and deadening certainties for their liveliness, their life, their ongoingness."[84]

Renewal, says Gadamer, is deeply rooted in an understanding that one's life is never finished and that our understanding "always must be renewed in the effort of our living."[85] This speaks to the notion that renewal must be at the heart of our work in understanding how schools learn together—and it is a call to school leaders to create space that allow for ongoing dialogue leading to transformative renewal. It is an understanding that nothing is permanent or fixed; some things become new again or they fade—nothing is final.

A New Metaphor: Ecology

A new language has been introduced into educational research. It emerged as a way to understand the complexity of educational endeavors and the interdependence of living relationships, the old and the new that exist within human systems. Within this new language is a shift from a mechanistic to an ecological worldview. The ecological metaphor recognizes that "the whole is more than the sum of its parts."[86] Thinking about the whole as both more and different from the compilation of individual parts is analogous to considering a mountain as differing from a pile of rocks; it is rather the enfolding of an entire landscape. Routine habits of mind, such as creating a timetable, need to be thought anew when individual's experience of learning is more than the assemblage of activities experienced through fragments of time.

The new ecological metaphor allows us to see the endeavor of schooling anew. And while it is easy to level criticism at the linear, factory-like precision model on which many school calendars and timetables operate, it is also important to acknowledge that the linear, lock-step model of schooling was propelled by a technological innovation—the assembly line—revolutionary and right for its time.

New ideas are needed for today. Educational researchers remind us, "To the extent that education becomes 'stuck' in ways of responding to the world that were once adequate to its demands, to that extent, it gradually becomes counter productive to the very responsiveness that is at its core."[87] And again: "What began with such enthusiasm and hope around a century ago in the organization and imagining of schooling has simply worn out."[88] According to Friesen and Jardine:

> Efforts to improve what are quickly becoming obsolete practices and structures are actually likely to make things worse. Many… administrators understand this issue first hand. Schools seemed to be continually accelerating, continually differentiating and multiplying the tasks that are asked of them, while, at the same time, attempting to leave in place the structures and practices that were responsive and responsible ventures over one hundred years ago. Exhaustion is the rule of the day. The good news is, however, that we are poised…for a genuine breakthrough in public education.[89]

My principal colleagues shared their experiences of renewal during our conversations. They provided deeper insight and an uncovering of these ideas to understand how school leaders who wish to create schools that learn might act differently to mirror the complex ecological relationships and processes that exist in nature.

Joe points out that the spirit of continuous learning, growth and renewal lives in every individual. With his observation "And I think if it's a dependent relationship where, I feed, you eat then that's when stuff live and die with one person [the leader]," Joe opens up the possibility of a new way for teachers and leaders to be together in schools that learn. What he suggests in creating a place where we learn from one another is a radical shift from the way schools have traditionally been structured. Individual "shopkeepers" who close their doors and carry out their professional responsibilities in isolation is the typical experience of teachers. An alternative way of learning together reflects Joe's vision where communities of adult learners can draw on the contributions of each member to engage the collective in developing a learning organization that inquires into their practice, learns from each other, and looks for evidence of impact on student achievement that moves their learning forward.[90] In this way of being together, deep engagement in learning is possible when conversations are undertaken within the context of living fields and where there exists the potential for advancement in understanding of how knowledge is actually cultivated.[91]

I've been given this opportunity to be one of the leaders in this school. We are on the journey together. There isn't one at the front. We want to continue to alternate taking places at the front so that you can learn from each other's failures. Now that I'm in it, I really enjoy the work, but team is everything.

I can't imagine doing that work if I didn't have a strong team that was willing to journey together, discover together, celebrate together, cry together. Because if you don't have that, then I think you can't do as well for kids, because anybody in isolation is never going to go as far as a group that's doing it together.

- Reia, School Principal

It Lives in Us All

This powerful possibility opens up when we value furtherance or renewal of processes, understanding, and knowledge. How do school leaders create a way of being, a school community that learns, that lives beyond the presence of the leader, the boss, the one controlling the school?

Reia and Joe acknowledge that their experience of leadership is more of a collective and not an individual who controls those being led. Joe shares the words *empowerment* and *ownership of learning*: learning not controlled by one individual, the leader, but lives in every individual. For her part, Reia spoke to the idea of leadership being a team endeavor with no one consistently in the lead position. Reia's comments provide insight into her thought that leadership is grounded in a position "at the front": "We want to continue to alternate taking places at the front, so that you can learn from each other, and anybody in isolation is never going to go as far as a group that's doing it together." However, in Reia's vision this position is shared, turns are taken, and no one is working in isolation. In a similar vein, Joe's comments suggest the responsibility and ownership of the work exist in everyone, all the time.

Their ideas are counter to how school leadership was defined in the early twentieth century. Robert Kanigal, professor of science writing at the Massachusetts Institute of Technology shares this about Taylor—who I previously described as one of the founders of standardized education: "In our scheme we do not ask for the initiative of our men. We do not want any initiative. All we want of them is to obey the orders we give them, do what we say, and do it quick. His declared purpose was to take all control from the hands of the workman (whom he regularly compared to oxen or horses) and place it in those of management."[92] As manifested in education, teachers and students are subjected to this loss of control: both do what they are told, in the sequence they are told to do it, and are assessed by those who will measure the efficiency of such work. Management historians and authors Charles Wrege and Ronald Greenwood describe the school system's orientation to a business model:

When it comes to leading, learning, and fostering learning from one another, it's very much not about me. It's very much not about any principal, assistant principal, or the Collaborative Teaching Partner or an expert being the passer on of the knowledge because that just fosters that same old script…"I'm a superhero who has the answer to everything" which I'm not and I don't.

And to be all things to all people is impossible for any one principal to be. Learning in our world today in inclusive environments, there's a lot of complexity. And so, the more flat an organization is, the more we can maximize tapping into people's strengths, passions, interest to allow opportunity for them to contribute so that the best ideas emerge to deal with the complexities.

- Joe, School Principal

In 1903, The Atlantic Monthly called for adoption of business organization by schools and William C. Bagley identified the ideal teacher as one who would rigidly "hew to the line." Bagley's ideal school was a place strictly reduced to rigid routine; he repeatedly stressed in his writing a need for "unquestioned obedience."[93]

In contrast, one can hear a new vision of leadership emerging in Joe and Reia's comments—a movement toward a shared leadership approach.

In the 1980s, educational researcher Philip Hallinger described an image of an instructional leader as one who used technical skills to coordinate and control, with the goal of aligning the school's academic mission with strategies and actions. This, he observed was the type of education leader that was gaining international interest and momentum in the 1980s. The responsibility of the leader was to focus not only on leading, but also on managing and included managerial tasks such as coordinating, controlling, and supervising curriculum and instruction. The focus, in this role, was on the control of teaching (i.e., evaluation) rather than on its development.[94] This image is not the kind of leadership the principals in my study were describing.

Yet, some developments may encourage that 1980s style of education leadership. For example, Alberta Education recently (2018) updated their Teaching Quality Standards (TQS). Will provincial attention to the TQS compel leaders to focus more on the evaluative aspects of their role as they seek to control and monitor teachers' classroom performances? There is also a risk that, in addition to the growing pains associated with implementing new policy, teachers may misinterpret the promotion of growth-oriented collegial interactions as breaches of their professional code of conduct; indeed, professional associations are quick to respond to such misinterpretations. On the other hand, are Reia and Joe suggesting that the leader no longer needs to look after their responsibility for ensuring quality teaching in every classroom? Or are they alluding to a shared responsibility for this important area of leadership? In this context, development of a shared approach to professional learning and growth is challenging.

Despite these challenges, to Reia this work, that of leading the learning in her school, is shared among the leadership team; Joe, on the other hand, hints at an even more widely decentralized network of leadership. Both suggest a leadership model that extends past the formal position of the school principal. For example, Joe talked about a flattened organization—a decentralized organizational network with no leader at the front—and called for complex leadership that is emergent, interactive, and dynamic. This concept of leadership is one where, as educational researchers Helen Timperley and Lorna Earl describe in their report on learning and change networks, the "activities and practices...are stretched over many people in a system of interactions that is more than the sum of the actions of individuals."[95] This suggests that everyone contributes and the whole is greater than the sum of the parts.

An ecological model such as Complex Adaptive Systems (CAS) may further understanding of a new concept of school leadership. The CAS is a framework for understanding how individual components of a collective interact when brought together. Emergent patterns of behavior are created from feedback loops throughout the system. These patterns are nonlinear forces of attraction. Examples of these nonlinear patterns of behavior can be found in collectives of ants, bees, brain cells, water particles in a weather pattern, groups of people in a city or town or school.[96] Learning within an organization, like classrooms or schools or a school system, follows nonlinear, complex processes like those of CAS.

Jardine sheds light on the ecological understanding of complex interactions and relationships that make it possible for learning to be owned by everyone and to live in every individual in a flattened organization. He shares this metaphor found in the Avatamsaka Sutra of Mahayana Buddhism, "Indra's Net":

Far away in the heavenly abode of the great god Indra, there is a wonderful net that has been hung by some cunning artificer in such a manner that it stretches out infinitely in all directions. In accordance with the extravagant tastes of deities, the artificer has hung a single glittering jewel in each "eye" of the net, and since the net itself is infinite in all dimensions, the jewels are infinite in number. There hang the jewels, glittering like stars of the first magnitude, a wonderful sight to behold. If we now arbitrarily select one of these jewels for inspection and look closely at it, we will discover that in its polished surface there are reflected all the other jewels in the net, infinite in number. Not only that, but each of the jewels reflected in this one jewel is also reflecting all the other jewels, so that there is an infinite reflecting process occurring.[97]

Jardine interprets "Indra's Net" as an awareness that we are all, each, present in each other, and are dependently co-arising. This is a deep ecology that speaks to a new paradigm in understanding schools as CAS. In this worldview, the world is seen as "an integrated whole rather than a dissociated collection of parts...[and] "recognizes the fundamental interdependence of all phenomena and the fact that, as individuals and societies, we're all embedded in (and ultimately dependent on) the cyclical processes of nature." [98]

A worldview of deep ecology that expands on the imagery created from "Indra's Net" is also captured in the following poem attributed to Chief Seattle, leader of the Suquamish and Duwamish Native American tribes. As a young warrior, Chief Seattle was known for his courage, daring and leadership. This is an excerpt from his speech, believed to have been given in 1854.

> This we know
> All things are connected
> Like the blood
> Which unites one family...
>
> Whatever befalls the earth,
> Befalls the sons and daughters of the earth.
> Man did not weave the web of life;
> He is merely a strand in it.
> Whatever he does to the web,
> He does to himself.[99]

How might an ecological lens help with understanding leadership differently? An ecological lens reflects what Joe shared when he said, "learning in our world today in inclusive environments, there's a lot of complexity that comes with that, and I don't have all the answers." When leadership is viewed through an ecological lens, it is seen less as a matter of hierarchical power and control and more as a flattened organizational structure. Nonlinear influence is spread across the network of individuals. This approach to leadership recognizes that the leader is one of many in the network and not the sole individual with all of the knowledge that the group needs at any given time. The interaction between the individuals provides the opportunity for knowledge building within the collective.

Davis and Sumara link complexity theories and deep ecology; the alignment between the two is understood within relationships and interactions. Specifically, they tell us, "knowledge is embodied or enacted in the ever-unfolding choreography of action within the universe. Stated bluntly, the truth isn't out there...what is known is acted out in what is done, and what is done contributes to the unfolding of the cosmos."[100] In other words, there is no fixed truth, no once-and-for-all answer that lives outside the continuous interaction between leaders, teachers, students, knowledge, and the context—it is always in dynamic motion—influencing, changing, and being influenced and changed by the other.

The complex interrelationships that exist in decentralized, scale-free networks—like those that exist in nature—provide a new lens for understanding a school community that learns together. Might this perspective provide some direction for how the school structures could be reconsidered in a renewal process that regenerates an enlivened network of relationships for learning and growth? Within this perspective, linear, structured progressions of learning outcomes give way to living connections of ideas; hierarchical grade structures give way to flexible groupings of learners who gather around topics for exploration; and traditional leadership models give way to a decentralized network of collaborative, interdependent professional staff who are invested in co-leading the school together.

A growing need exists for teaching professionals to create interdependent collaborative cultures. James Surowiedki, author of *The Wisdom of Crowds*, observes, "As science has become ever more specialized and as the number of subfields within each discipline has proliferated, it's become difficult for a single person to know everything he needs to know."[101] Similarly, too much is going on for a single school leader to be expected to know everything they need to know. A turn toward a decentralized leadership paradigm, as in a complex adaptive system that exists in nature, might provide the foundation for collective learning and leading that potentially lives in every individual.

This can be understood through the concept of neighboring interactions that exist naturally in a social collective.

Within this concept, the learning of a group is a trans-level phenomenon. This means that if a social collective can expand their ability to find novel new ways to address complex problems that arise in the schools and classrooms of the twenty-first century, then the individuals that comprise the collective must each individually learn and adapt.[102] In this way, individual interests and collective interests are not in competition; rather, it is possible to nurture individual capacity when collective potential is strengthened because anybody in isolation will never go as far as a group doing it together.

For Reflection

Chapter Six: Networks of Influence

1. What processes are in place to let go of old practices to make way for the new?

2. What evidence or research provides the support for a different approach? How do you initiate the change?

3. What do you see as areas where change is needed? How will you engage your school community in seeing that change is needed?

4. How have networks of influence been created within your school community? Within your district?

Chapter Seven

Collective Leadership

To lead people walk behind them.

- Lao Tzu

What does it mean to be a leader within a collaborative decentralized network?

September 2015

Today I open the door to a space provided by my superintendent. It is my new office. It's not in a school. It is in my school district's central office building. It feels strange to not be in a school this September. How will I be in this very different environment? I walked through the doors and into a school every September since I was five years old. I miss my school community!

I said yes when my superintendent asked me to become the division principal for our school district. What is a division principal? I don't know for sure. My superintendent doesn't know for sure. He says we will figure it out together. He tells me I will be working with other principals in our district. I am very excited about this. I imagine I will be helping them create learning that matters for their students and their teachers. I am also starting my doctoral program at the University of Calgary. I will be learning more about leadership in K–12 schools. I am very excited about this, too. I imagine I can apply my new learning to this new role as a division principal. I imagine I will continue to learn with this collective of principals that leadership matters in schools where learning matters. I hope to be inspired by the work of my principal colleagues so I might deepen my understanding of what it means to lead well within our schools.

The meaning of the word *leader* comes from the Old English word lǣdere: "any person who leads or directs." The word *lead* is also derived from Old English and means "to guide, cause to go with oneself; march at the head of, go before as a guide, accompany and show the way; carry on; sprout forth, bring forth."[103] Leading as a guide, to accompany, might provide a way to understand leadership in a complex adaptive system where the leader does not take a position in front but, perhaps, walks beside or supports the bringing forth in others humbly from behind.

Leadership might also be understood as something that requires everyone to recognize that each individual does not have all the answers but, together, each individual's contribution can propel the group forward to create new ways to respond to complex problems or situations, such as those within today's classrooms and schools. An ecological paradigm provides opportunities for creative solutions to unfold throughout a learning collective that is open, thriving, sprouting forth from fertile ground. Again, as Lao Tzu suggested,

"A leader is best when people barely know he exists, when his work is done, his aim fulfilled, they will say: we did it ourselves."

A teacher shared this quote with me and said this was who I was as a leader. It was a moment when I was given the rare opportunity to see myself reflected in the observation of another. While I recognize this is the way one individual saw my leadership, her words have remained with me. Its message has continued to shape my leadership practice.

Moments in one's lived experience arrive unexpectedly and out of all proportion. These moments forever shape how one sees themselves. The obligation, the choices about what to do with the words gifted to me, belonged only to me. I was now responsible to what had been given. It was addressed to me by hands not my own. My intention, perhaps more tacit than explicit, to be a leader who walked beside others, who did not lead from a "positional" model of power, compliance, and control was being affirmed by a colleague.

My intention was never to become the formal leader of a school. All I really ever wanted for myself in my career as a teacher was to harness the power of team to bring out the best in each other and our students. In my experience as a multi-age team teacher and as a hockey mom, I witnessed the magic created when a well-coached team understands that every player has a unique and necessary strength to contribute to the team; the team achieves far more success than a team of individual super heroes. This experience contributed to the principles that have guided my way of being when I took on the role of school principal. I still remember the conversation between my principal and I as she shared with me the news she was leaving our school community to take on a new leadership role in our district. I was thrilled for her. She deserved this new opportunity. She served our school and school district for so many years as a confident yet compassionate leader with a strong vision for what kind of education our learners deserved. She was my cheerleader and a source of inspiration for me. Her encouragement led me to venture out, beyond the walls of my classroom, to explore the unfamiliar role of school administrator. Now, my rock, my mentor, my safety net was leaving, and as assistant principal, I was terrified! Who would replace her? Would we be allowed to continue with the vision and goals we had just started to bring to life in our school community. Should I apply for the position of principal at our school? I do not want to be a principal; it is not who I am. I needed to decide. I remember my principal, once again, encouraging me to step up and take on this role. She believed in my ability to lead a school community long before I believed it of myself.

I was shaken to the core. To me, the word *principal* implied formal leadership. The meaning I associated with the word principal was expert, boss, manager, one at the front. None of these words conjured up anything that fit with who I believed myself to be and what I saw for myself as an educator. Forget it! I am not that person and I do not want to become that person. I want to continue to be the person who works alongside others, who asks questions, problem-solves with others, challenges the thinking of others, welcomes my thinking to be challenged, engages in conversations with colleagues about what we might do together to move forward with our learning. A principal is expected to have the answers, right? The principal needs to be seen as confident, capable, strong, and knowledgeable. This was not who I was. I knew that no matter what my role in a school, I needed to be seen for who I truly was: not someone with everything figured out but, instead, someone who is a learner. How could anyone who openly expressed to others that they do not have all the answers ever hope to pull off the role of school principal?

Then something changed. I thought about the work that my principal and I had done to create a collaborative school community. We were a long way from having anything figured out, once-and-for-all (in a complex organization, there is no once-and-for-all); however, all of our teachers had their feet pointed in the same direction and we were moving forward together. Something we had established within the first two years of opening our new school was the creation of a design team of teacher leaders representing every grade level in the school. We were establishing a way of learning together, with our design team, that would serve as a model for how each team of educators in the school would learn and work together. A leadership team was in place that could guide and support each other to lead the school.

The existence of our design team turned out to be the reason I applied for the position of school principal. I knew that with the collective leadership of our design team, I would not need to be all things to all people. I would never be alone with the responsibility of leading the school community.

I wanted to shift the way leadership was enacted at my school, as a team of many, each assuming leadership roles. As it evolved, my office team grew and more teachers took on leadership roles: an assistant principal, a technology lead, a learning coach, and an inclusive education lead, and we continued to nurture leadership among the teachers.

This team approach to leadership is described in the research literature using diverse leadership terms: distributed, shared, or collaborative. The spreading out of leadership is something each principal in my study referred to during their interviews. The leadership they described created opportunities for different leaders to emerge.

Leadership emerges in an interconnected network of neighbors; considering how neighbors interact with each other in a complex organization is important. Neighbors are not only physical bodies or social groupings but also "the neighbors that must interact with one another are ideas, hunches, queries, and other manners of representation."[104] This illuminates Reia's comment: "anybody in isolation is never going to go as far as a group that's doing it together." Reia's acknowledgement of the importance of connectedness can be extended even further by recognizing that the connectedness refers to people and their ideas. Leaders who seek to create ongoing renewal among their staff members are not only aware of this important dynamic, but they also create opportunities for the networking to happen so it is not about control of the process. Reia and the others all discussed how they intentionally create opportunities for staff to gather together, formally and informally. It is through these gatherings "that ideas will stumble across one another." [105]

Davis and Sumara go on to say that one of the most important features of neighboring is that throughout the interactions "one must relinquish any desire to control the structure and outcomes of the collective."[106] This has significant implications for leading a school community that learns. Within a structure-determined complex system, external authorities cannot impose; they merely create the conditions, the fertile ground. The system itself decides what is and is not acceptable.

Regarding shared/distributed work or understanding, the outcome is that a person should never strive to position herself or himself as the final authority on matters of appropriate or correct action. This would be a considerable shift from traditional leadership models. This shift is emerging in the schools that the three principals are leading. They shared their goal of creating schools that learn where the adult learners are taking ownership of their learning to influence and improve student learning and solve complex challenges within their school communities.

Individuals cannot be separated from each other or their environment. We are, individually, all interconnected and interdependent. This is why change lives in us all. What happens to one happens to all. As the thirteenth-century Sufi poet Rumi observed:

You are not a drop in the ocean
You are the entire ocean in a drop.

This shift from growth, learning, and change from individual to collective implies an ongoing dance that proceeds through a subtle interplay of competition and cooperation, creation, and mutual adaptation. It is a collective, networked, ecological process that recognizes the interdependence of individuals within their contexts.

Capra tells us, "Throughout the living world evolution cannot be limited to the adaptation of organisms to their environment, because the environment itself is shaped by a network of living systems capable of adaptation and creativity."[107] In other words, one does not adapt to the other; they co-evolve. Understanding from nature this process of continual growth and adaptation helps to conceive of the classroom or school as a complex network of interdependent relationships that are changing both the individuals and the collective. The knowledge and the learning live in individuals and individuals live in the collective. This co-evolution helps to shed light on the understanding that the sum of the collective is more than just a collection of individuals. Understanding this concept provides a lens for understanding how learning is emergent, highly contextual, and can be owned by no one individual (i.e., leader).

If leaders recognize the complex nature of the relationships for learning within their school context, and trust that the same natural processes that exist in nature also exist in social systems, they may loosen their tendencies to control the learning of their teachers from a position of authority. What might this mean for teachers who learn collectively? How might leaders decentralize control and adopt the concept of co-evolution to engage teachers in not only their individual learning but meaningful, authentic learning of the collective? How might this learning across the entire school organization improve student learning?

Educational researchers Leyton Schnellert and Deborah Butler describe the importance of the social collective in teachers' professional learning.[108] Through a process of collaborative inquiry, teachers can collectively define problems, co-plan, co-teach, co-monitor, and interpret outcomes to consider what's next. When teachers embed their professional learning in the context of their work, recognizing the complex interplay between the individual, the collective and the environment, they are learning as they teach together, as a collective. This may be a way for teacher learning to live in individuals and to benefit from the emergence of creative possibilities that develop from the collective when, as Joe pointed out, this is not just my class; all kids in our school are all our kids. We are all inextricably linked, there is a unity, a wholeness; we are one, learning together.

Unity and togetherness, in the sense of being one, is reflected in routines and structures within a community. The circular structure is customary in Indigenous cultures. For thousands of years, Indigenous peoples used healing or talking circles to deal with personal and emotional matters. The circle embraces and teaches the traditional values of respect, care and non-interference. It represents the holism of Mother Earth and the equality of all members. In some groups, a stone is passed from speaker to speaker, symbolizing the connection among group members and to the guiding spirit. The holder of the object speaks from the heart, and the group listens silently and non-judgmentally until the speaker has finished. Each member is given a chance to speak. A common rule of circle work is that members must not speak out of turn. The circle structure actually affected communication patterns when students were moved from a holistic circle structure to a linear one revealing the significance of the structure of the circle.[109]

I remember a university class from my masters program where this same circle structure was incorporated. My professor talked at length about the significance of the circle structure in ensuring everyone had a voice and every member of the circle could be seen and heard; there was never a time when we were speaking to the back of someone's head, which typically happens when we gather in rows or table groups. In this way, the relationship is strengthened by ensuring eye contact and the undivided attention of everyone in the group.

My professor also shared that the circle provides a strong sense of belonging and connection as we gather together, beside each other, with no one at the front. I used this structure often with my staff, particularly at the end of the school year when we came together to share experiences, highlights, and challenges from the year. I found it fascinating that this structure actually made some staff members uncomfortable as it often led to some very emotional sharing. Teachers often used the circle structure within their classrooms, with several incorporating Socratic Circles into their practice. My observation of this practice was that it made students far more relaxed and deepened the conversations; it felt more personal.

There are going to be people who need to step into our shoes and so we're always trying to build leadership. A lot of times we're asking several of these staff members to present, to speak intentionally at large group meetings.

So, when they do that it builds less of an us and them mentality. They're seeing a lot of learning coming from their peers. An example recently was Indigenous circles. We put the whole staff in one great big circle for the staff meeting and then one grade five teacher got up and talked about why we did this, why this is so important.

- Christine, School Principal

Christine's choice to incorporate this circle structure with her staff may represent her intention to create a space that feels safe for dialogue where individuals feel connected and trust in the relationships between individuals is strengthened. Small acts, like the seating arrangement in a staff meeting, signal the desire to renew traditional practices and structures of a school community providing a space *to place new steps of change*. Something as simple as a circular seating plan can bring a community of learners closer, create a sense of belonging. Through this more personal structure, it becomes possible to have the *grace to look up and out and into your sister's eyes, into your brother's face*.

Creating opportunities for others to lead the learning of staff, as Christine points out, is a practical example of the collective leadership model where others are encouraged to join in. Friesen, in personal communication, May 2018, shares that leadership, when seen through the lens of a complex, ecological metaphor, can be described as "finding ways for leadership throughout;

because there is openness, different and new people can come forward; you can work on new ideas that are not owned by any individual. Ideas are held by the collective. This allows different people to emerge as leaders."

In a school community that learns, it is possible for leaders to emerge from within the school setting. This plays out in schools when leaders provide space, time, and opportunities within the collective for colleagues to contribute their knowledge and experience to the collective learning of the whole. When this becomes the learning culture of the school, ideas are not owned by individuals but, instead, become shared by the group.

School, as conceived within an ecological metaphor, is not about any one thing. It is about the complex interconnectedness of all living things: the culture of a school and all the individuals and their relationships to themselves, each other, and the school community. Their growth is not an individual matter but inextricably intertwined within the growth of others. *Whatever he does to the web, he does to himself.*

What stands in the way of making this way of being together a reality in more schools? Is this shift from a traditional hierarchical organization even possible within a society or a school system that seeks to hold individuals, not collectives, responsible for missteps or mistakes? I am reminded of a meeting with my superintendent and his senior executive team when immediate access to principals was being discussed. It was determined the principal, and only the principal, was to ensure they were available by cell phone when the superintendent was calling. I asked if this was an expectation, even if the principal was, for example, in the dentist's chair?

It is this mindset, one that sees only one individual holding the sole responsibility for the organization, that creates a barrier to a more distributed, networked organizational model. Those who hold fast to traditional management structures surely believe that chaos would ensue if the single power position within an organization was abdicated in favour of a networked, collaborative team approach. If a flattened structure existed, who would be held accountable if students were not performing? Where would the angry, disappointed parents go to voice their concerns? Who would the superintendent call when a board member becomes disgruntled after hearing rumours within the community about a particular school or teacher?

Is it at all realistic to believe that schools or districts could flatten their pecking orders so much that no one individual would be held ultimately responsible when assurance and accountability are required? Are we not all collectively responsible for our commitments, decisions, and actions? Might it be possible to shift the recognition and the blame to the integrated whole community that is in this together?

What steps might be taken to help individuals realize what shared commitment, responsibility, and contribution to the collective leadership of a school could look like? I remember a time, early in my principalship, when I first attempted to answer this question. The step I took was to invite staff, who often complained about the timetable, to join me and my assistant principal before the start of the school year as we co-created the timetable. A few teachers joined us and, through this collaborative scheduling process, they saw the complexity involved in deciding about how to best organize the people and spaces available so the conditions for the best possible learning for all students—not just the students in their classrooms—could be created.

While this process was time consuming, it provided my assistant principal and me an opportunity to understand more deeply how our decisions were affecting teachers while also providing us with insights from the fresh eyes of our teachers. It was during such informal collaborative meetings that an understanding and respect for each other's responsibilities was deepened within the school community.

Ultimately, although a leader might extend the network of leadership and share many responsibilities that come with leading a school community, they will always be the individual with the authority to make final decisions and will be held accountable for those decisions that affect the work taking place within the school. Naively believing this will change soon is futile; however, accepting this ultimate responsibility—while also understanding the value of drawing on the exceptional human resources of a strong team—elevates the collective work of the organization. It provides much-needed sources for renewal within the school.

A leader is only as good as the people they surround themselves with. This is what it means to lead collectively, within a collaborative organization. A leader needs to understand that no matter how much the work is shared, a line in the sand defines who is ultimately responsible. This belongs to no one else but the lone school principal. While decentralized leadership may provide opportunities for co-evolutionary renewal to emerge where the collective is in this together, the decision to enact a non-hierarchical school organization rests with the individual, the brave warrior, who recognizes this form of leadership is not the familiar, the safe, nor the easily understood.

The school principal who chooses to lead this way suffers judgment from the top for giving away power to others, judgment from within for shirking responsibilities and further burdening teachers, and judgment from the outside for choosing not to be the one in front with all the answers. When a leader is courageous enough to put processes in place that support a loosening of control, the opportunity might then exist to recognize that "order emerges from interactions having just the right amount of tension or difference or imbalance among the elements interacting." [110] The elements interacting are students, teachers, leaders, and ideas. When a school community that learns together is engaged in this kind of dynamic learning, there might indeed be space *to place new steps of change*.

For Reflection

Chapter Seven: Collective Leadership

1. How has leadership been distributed within your context?

2. What are the challenges of a distributed leadership model? What is working well? How do you know?

3. How is decision making shared? What has been effective with this approach? What has been challenging?

Chapter Eight

Spreading Seeds

All living systems start small. Each of us once began as an embryo, smaller than a fingernail. The mighty sequoia tree begins in the humblest seed. It is no different in growing a new organizational culture. Once we surrender the myth that a "heroic CEO creates change," we understand that all great things have small beginnings and we begin thinking naturally in terms of "pilot groups."

- Peter Senge, Systems Scientist

What if we could spread what works through networks of influence?

September 2005

Today we open the doors to a space built on a dream for middle years learners; those students who are often described as the most difficult to reach and teach. Our school district was ready to rethink the traditional struc-
ture of the junior high school setting with its "pop tart" time tables; pop in for 45 minutes, pop out to the next chunk of learning, isolated class-rooms, and fragmented subjects. I had been selected as the assistant principal charged with co-designing this brand-new school for learners in grades five through nine. I had learned so much from my experience in the multi-age program; I was ready to spread what worked from that classroom to a whole school context with our young adolescent learners.

The parents of our youngest, bright-eyed, energetic grade five and six students were not convinced that restructuring the grade configurations of the schools within our city was a good idea. These parents worried about their children being mixed in with the unruly teenagers who were traditionally separated from the children and shipped off to "junior high school grade seven to nine factories" during the school day—where these teens lived out of lockers and moved from class to class when the bell signaled the end of one disconnected learning bit and the start of another, trying to keep the homework assignments sorted out and ready for submission to one of the eight to ten teachers they saw throughout the week. Now, their precious, innocent grade five and six students who previously attended the K–6 schools in our city would be forced to mix with the teenagers in grades seven to nine as we brought all these children together in our new grades five to nine middle school.

Previously, the only time the young, impressionable grades five and six children were exposed to these foreign hormonal influences was on the school bus ride, in the malls, at their sports and recreational activities, during family get-togethers with cousins, or at home every evening around the dinner table. What turns us around like this, only able to see one way of organizing for learning? How would we ever convince these parents that the team teaching, flexible learning spaces, inquiry and collaborative group work would provide their children with learning that matters to them? How could we shine a light on the students' most meaningful learning experiences, the times they unearthed new understanding about the world around them and their connection to it, when they contributed to a community of learning, re-discovering their innate curiosity, and building knowledge together? All that our parents could see right now was there were NO DESKS placed in "cemetery seating" arrangements; desk after desk, row after row, like headstones of the dead lined up in a graveyard. Instead, our school provided only tables for our students so they could learn from and with each other.

We also provided flexible spaces for learning with walls that opened up to expand the classrooms into team teaching spaces. All the parents could see right now was a school breaking tradition. How could this be good for their kids? We would likely feel the pressure from our parent community for some time. How could we win them over?

In her renewal efforts at her school, Christine spent the past two years "test[ing] the waters" in creating the conditions for collaboration among her teachers. Christine is intent on rejuvenating her school's process for professional learning and recognizes that through ongoing collaboration, her staff can enter into a continuous learning model with colleagues.

The first year, she had a single team of teachers start small with a group inquiry and dedicated time to learning together. Christine shared enthusiastically how the excitement and interest in teacher collaboration spread among the staff. She witnessed, first hand, the vitality created from providing the fertile ground to nurture live encounters among her staff. From this humble beginning, Christine's entire staff became interested in testing the waters of collaboration during the following school year. How did this small spark spread so quickly among Christine's staff?

Some of them have never collaborated. I'm not so sure this is the year that we say there shall be an agenda and there needs to be an action plan and everything else.

It had to be a little more of let's just test the waters in giving them a couple of half days to get together with a focus. It isn't very structured this year. Will I know exactly what the benefits of the collaboration are by the end of this year? No. But will I know they have tested collaboration and that they're very much supporting each other in something? Then I'm happy.

I would imagine next year our goal would be come and meet with me. Let me know how your collaboration went. What did you get out of it? Why is it worth us setting some money aside for you to get together?

- Christine, School Principal

A favorite author from my childhood, Lucy Maude Montgomery, reminds us in her story *Anne of Green Gables*: "All things great are wound up with all things little."[111] All things great start small, the greater whole is embodied in all things little. This is how phenomena exist in nature. How might the study of nature deepen the understanding of humble beginnings? How does this live within the renewal of a school community?

Concepts from Nature

Through an ecological lens on the natural world, concepts of self-similarity and fractal forms can shed light on the potential that exists in studying smaller parts in relation to the whole of a complex system. These smaller fractal forms possess self-similar qualities to that of the whole and can open up understanding of the whole. Fractal forms can, with surprising detail, emerge from simple beginnings and, when extended to learning contexts, suggest a way of understanding how learners can elaborate on simple experiences and understandings that transform their thinking into more elaborate insights, sometimes very quickly. A complex pattern of organization is at play here: the understanding present in the individual, or part, is also evident in the complete whole. An understanding of the individual, or component part, can lead to an expanded understanding of the whole; self-similar patterns are in both the part and the whole.[112]

Fractal images exhibit the quality of self-similarity in that one can be made to fit exactly on top of the other; the parts resemble the wholes and enlarging a part will produce an image that closely matches the original figure. Self-similar forms demonstrate that complexity is not a function of scale. The same level of detail presents itself in the smaller part as in the whole.

Value can be found in examining the part as a representation of the whole. However, such partial viewings could never adequately provide a full understanding of the larger form. Rather, what is important to note is that partial studies are no simpler and no less informative than studies of the whole. By examining the complex particulars of smaller pieces, the fractal images, an understanding of patterns that comprise the whole can emerge.

Through this interpretation of complex collectives and their self-similar characteristics, the boundaries for organizing these smaller parts are never tidy or fixed. Further, each layer or body can be simultaneously seen as a whole, a part of a whole, or as a complex compilation of smaller wholes. This understanding transfers to the importance of studying the particulars of the school and classroom to gain a deeper understanding of the whole. Through the concept of self-similarity, the particulars of interpreting the actions of this student, in this classroom, with this teacher, and on this day offer the potential to shine a light of understanding on the larger whole of the system. The classroom is a microcosm of the school.

For a special collection of forms, parts resemble the wholes. Enlarging a well-chosen piece will generate an image that closely matches the original figure—and this is a quality manifest in many natural forms including fern fronds, cauliflower, parsley, clouds, riverbeds, trees, water ripples, and coastlines. Further, the complexity within systems such as schools is not necessarily a function of scale; when applying the characteristic of self-similarity to a dynamic school community, "the sorts of nested phenomena are suggested to operate and unfold in similar ways."[113] By exploring parts of the system and studying the dynamics, we can learn more about the whole system.

Humble Beginnings: Pilots and Prototypes

The concept of fractal forms may shine a light of understanding into what is at play when testing the waters in a small pilot situation. A pilot becomes a natural way to flexibly explore creative ideas that might be expanded to other classrooms and organizational structures within the school. This process may contribute to renewal within a school community that furthers processes and structures so it feels less risky than wholesale change. It allows for more gradual exploration of smaller initiatives.

Reia explores the complexity of a decentralized system where emergence of new ideas is bottom-up, emergent, or grass-rooted. Within her school, the renewal of teaching practices is being studied in smaller parts to better understand how the learning might ripple out to the rest of her staff. Is starting small and just hoping for the interactions between neighbors enough to spark the spread of renewal and innovation or is something more needed? Is Reia's intention to have learning be grass-rooted connected to Joes's comments about change processes *living in individuals?* Are they both referring to the same concept: that of ownership and engagement in learning as opposed to something mandated from one in an authority position?

This is a similar dynamic to what exists within a classroom buzzing with curiosity and a desire to explore and discover. Can the same understanding of authentic, engaged learning from classrooms apply to the learning of teachers, where they are inspired, collectively, to learn together? Will this collective learning provide insight into answering Reia's million-dollar question: "How do we take a structure and now apply it into a different area of the school?"

Clearly, so much can be learned from starting small: studying humble beginnings; and looking for patterns, structures, and connections that can help us understand how these patterns might inform other areas of the school. However, as complexity teaches us, there are no simple solutions and the unique characteristics of students, staff, and the context in another part of the school might not allow for a neat and tidy application of new learning.

Renewal experiences that rely on experimentation and prototyping to explore big ideas in a small-scale way to study them, get feedback, make early adjustments, and redesign better solutions are how David Kelley, founder of the global design and innovation company IDEO and Stanford University professor, with his brother Tom Kelley, test the waters of innovation continuously in their work at IDEO and the Stanford design school. Starting small can allow designers to expand on key design features that can then be replicated on a broader scale.[114]

This design principle plays out in a school environment in much the same way as the principals described their small-scale experiments with new teaching practices and organizational models for collaboration. They are seeing the self-similarity that exists in a complex system as an opportunity to start small: examine the complex network of interactions, structures, and processes; and study what works to discover what might be possible in a larger context across nested layers within learning organizations.

Successful organizations employ specific qualities when establishing a collective commitment to change that sees an expansion of renewal spread

> The learning leaders at my school are just getting into all eight of each other's classrooms, with a discussion after-hours of what they're seeing.
>
> Our hope for our next step is to find out how we take a structure that we know is getting results and apply it to a different area of the school?
>
> So, there's already a lot of excitement around the writers' workshop as well as this readers' reciprocal teaching. Our grade 6 team is so excited; so, we're going to be implementing it in their classrooms. We're looking for ways for this to be grass-rooted.
>
> **- Reia, School Principal**

beyond the initial "pilot group." Many of these ideas strike a familiar chord with the qualities that comprise authentic learning for students:

- Connect with real work goals and processes;
- Involve people who have the autonomy to act regarding the goals;
- Provide increased opportunities for people to think and reflect without pressure to decide;
- Develop people's individual and collective capacity;
- Focus on learning about learning, in settings that matter;
- Balance action and reflection along with a connection between inquiry and experimentation.[115]

A culture of experimentation, change, learning, and growth is connected to the essence of deep ecology: ask deeper questions. Within an ecological metaphor, we need to be prepared to question every single aspect of the old paradigm. Capra says that deep ecology

> asks profound questions about the very foundations of our modern, scientific, industrial, growth-oriented, materialistic worldview and way of life. It questions this entire paradigm from an ecological perspective: from the perspective of our relationships to one another, to future generations, and to the web of life of which we are part.[116]

This is a challenging space to lead from, and not one highly supported among the public who look to schools as places of stability, security, and predictability. Prototyping new processes to create the conditions for student learning are not yet received well by parents who do not want their children to be experimental guinea pigs.

I remember vividly the public dissent that took over our small community when the doors to the new experimental middle school were opened. Curious parents and students were provided with early tours to see how learning would look different within this school community: What…no desks?! What…double-wide classrooms with folding walls?! What…team teaching?!

Parents were not convinced that the changes to the traditional school setting would see their children set up for success during their remaining years in school and in the world beyond school. We persevered. Some families left. Some staff left. Those who remained became our strongest supporters and those most committed to ensuring we continued to be trail blazers, explorers, and innovators. We turn now to understanding schools that learn through a continual cycle of renewal that begins with asking questions.

For Reflection

Chapter Eight: Spreading Seeds

1.   Can you identify a time when you prototyped a new idea? What were the advantages of this approach? What were the disadvantages? What did you learn from this experience?

2.   In what ways do you encourage others to "test the waters" of change?

3.   How were you able to spread the seeds of new learning to others within the school community? The school district? Beyond the school community? Beyond the school district?

Chapter Nine

Living the Questions

Here where I am surrounded by an enormous landscape which the winds move across as they come from the seas, here I feel there is no one anywhere who can answer for me these questions and feelings which, in their depths, have a life of their own...have patience with everything unresolved in your heart and try to love the questions themselves, as if they were locked rooms or books written in a very foreign language. Don't search for the answers, which could not be given to you now, because you would not be able to live them. And the point is to live everything. Live the questions now. Perhaps then some day far into the future, you will gradually without even noticing it, live your way to the answers.

- Rainer Maria Rilke, from "Letters to a Young Poet"

What if we could re-awaken our natural curiosity?

September 1997

Today we open the doors to a brand-new space that my teacher colleagues and I designed. We were given the freedom and support to re-imagine learning for the students in our care. Our multi-age classroom had been constructed within our traditional school setting.

Within this space there were a pod of computers, a loft, an open concept design, and even a kitchen! Three grade levels of students and a four-teacher team would attempt to design powerful learning that matters for our primary aged students. The children would be important members of our learning community; one stood out from the rest. I could not let this teaching "experiment" fail him or the others. My investment in this became deeply personal. My youngest son, Brett, was in this class. He, like many other curious, active children, did not LOVE school. He LOVED recess! He LOVED playing! He LOVED riding his bike through the forest with his older brother, making forts, capturing frogs to bring home and look at. Could we keep these curious young minds deeply engaged in learning that matters to them?

We had more questions than answers as we jumped into a graduate level course together to explore project-based learning with Dr. Sylvia Chard at the University of Alberta. It was over twenty years ago when my school principal approached my multi-age teaching team and asked us to consider deepening our understanding of what it meant to use student questions to drive learning. We were novices, inexperienced in how we would open up the curriculum for exploration by students instead of continuing our known and comfortable practice of a one-way delivery method of "I teach, you learn" teacher-centered pedagogy. I remember our confusion as we dove into an inquiry approach to teaching. We questioned ourselves, our ability to teach this way and we questioned why we were beginning our studies with so many student questions! A few of our ongoing questions were:

- What is it with all these questions?
- Why do we keep asking the kids to come up with questions?
- What are we supposed to do with all these questions?
- I don't get it: do they all answer all these questions?
- Do we group the questions?
- Do we eliminate the easy-to-look-up questions?
- Do we teach them about what a good question is?

We began together, with a small, experimental, created space for change, and set out on one of the most significant learning adventures of our careers. We were seeking to renew our teaching methods by opening up to the potential that a different, innovative approach might provide. The key that seemed to unlock the mystery of a student-owned and more engaging experience in learning was a shift in focus to a continual process of renewal; we recognized we would never, really, be experts in a constantly changing landscape of learning and learners. We began our journey into a new way of being with each other and our students as we explored how questioning would sustain in-depth inquiry and spark curiosity.

Amateur Researchers

"Try to love the questions themselves." This shift in thinking was powerful in transforming our classroom teaching practice. Learning to love the questions themselves, to be comfortable in the world of mystery that exists everywhere, waiting to be uncovered, and finding inspiration in all that remains to be solved might be what opens possibility for the continual renewal that exists in a school community that learns. Echoes from my past, from the voice of Anne, my childhood literary heroine, painted a vivid picture of what it means to be curious and open to wonder in the story *Anne of Green Gables*:

So teachers need to be amateur researchers. They need to be seeking those answers out for themselves. What it often takes is learning coaches and administrators to guide them and just ask them: why don't you try reading this or why don't you try looking at this or why don't you go visit that class? Help them kind of navigate this world of feeling like a qualified teacher.

- Christine, School Principal

Isn't it splendid to think of all the things there are to find out about? It just makes me feel glad to be alive—it's such an interesting world. It wouldn't be half so interesting if we knew all about everything, would it? There'd be no scope for imagination then, would there?[117]

I embraced this mindset as a teacher and felt compelled to ensure that through my teaching practice, I nurtured the wonder and curiosity that innately exists in our children. As a leader, I came to understand this same curious disposition would also propel the continuous learning and growth of our teachers. The principals I interviewed for my dissertation research revealed a similar awareness.

All three leaders spoke to the culture of questioning they are creating among their teachers, the *amateur researchers*. They are modelling, for their staff, how to learn to love the questions themselves as a way to engage in a continuous learning process, to engage in inquiry, like a researcher always seeking new learning and contributing to building new knowledge. Christine's comment about feeling like a qualified teacher caught me off guard and got me thinking, wondering, curious. How can an amateur researcher navigate this world of feeling like a qualified teacher? I wonder about how one ever feels like a qualified teacher. What is a qualified teacher? And how do any of us become one?

> So, the way that sort of lives out is, not trying to be a dictator. So a lot of shared decision making, input, feedback, and a lot of "what do you think?"
>
> Sometimes that's informal and other times that's staff meeting more formally.
>
> **- Joe, School Principal**

What is a Qualified Teacher? A Case Study from Alberta

In an example I provided earlier, I referred to Alberta Education's revised TQS, which outlines what it means to be a qualified teacher in the province of Alberta. This guideline is for teachers and the leaders who are tasked with the responsibility of nurturing teacher growth and judging their success in meeting the Standard through processes outlined for leaders within Alberta in the Teacher Growth, Supervision, and Evaluation Policy (TGSEP). The TGSEP requires that leaders engage in ongoing supervision and evaluation of teachers.[118] It places an important responsibility on school leaders for judging and deciding about what it means to be a *qualified teacher.*

The TGSEP requires that leaders use the TQS to determine if teachers are qualified in an ever-changing complex school environment. The list of competencies, and qualifying indicators in the TQS provides direction for leaders; its function is akin to a compass to navigate the shifting sands of complexity that exist when trying to determine quality in an ever-changing context. The list, in some ways, attempts to simplify this complexity, distill it down into an easily understood, manageable list of competencies that, if successfully demonstrated, would ensure that a teacher can feel like a qualified teacher, able to confidently navigate the waters of change, that exist in the everyday experience of their professional lives.

How can that be true in a complex system? An understanding of the interconnected social networks and continuously changing learning landscape in a school community that learns requires recognition that being and becoming a qualified teacher is not a state of arrival. Nor is it a checklist of knowledge, skills, attitudes, or competencies that signal becoming a qualified teacher. Rather, greater complexity is at play here. In an environment where change is constant and new learning shapes both the learner and the context—while the learner continues to change the known—it

Any time my assistant principal and I were able to attend the alternative professional development, it was the questioning that we would provide that I think helped validate certain things that they were doing, as well as question some of the things they thought were either going well or not well. So the three of us were brainstorming: "What's our next mini-lesson?" "How are we seeing kids respond to this?" "How are we making this stronger?" "Do we have evidence that this is actually working?" We'd be getting goose bumps, because of some of the discussion that was coming out of these kids. We're really celebrating that and we've done it in a way that my assistant principal and I intentionally planned. We would plop in for a couple weeks, but pull out, and it would still run itself.

- Reia, School Principal

is very difficult to understand how this can be a once-and-for-all arrival at being a qualified teacher. A shared understanding of what a teacher and or leader needs to know, be, and do is required for setting professional learning goals; however, these may need to be open to continual renewal and adjustment based on evolving knowledge and context.

Perhaps the only competency that really is a once-and-for-all in the new standard for teachers and leaders is one that describes a process of lifelong learning. This competency aligns with the curious disposition that Christine,

Reia, and Joe are nurturing among their staff. Specifically, these leaders address the following competency indicators:

- Collaborating with other teachers to build personal and collective professional capacities and expertise
- Actively seeking feedback to enhance teaching practice
- Seeking, critically reviewing, and applying educational research to improve practice

Might a continuous cycle of inquiry into professional practice, inspired from within and propelled forward in response to natural curiosity, be a more promising way to create a school community that learns? Would a collaborative collective of professionals who learn from and with each other provide an alternative to the outdated, top-down, managerial leadership model where external judgment and evaluation of performance is the driver for improving the learning for all?

I think that professional learning is an ongoing and constant process more than it is a specific event. You know, we share research, we share videos. We are walking down the road of how we get feedback, and how we know if what we're doing is working. Some of the conversations that we're having are: "Let's bring student work to the table to see what we're getting from our lessons. What are we we seeing in what the students are producing?"

And I think having those conversations around student work is a little less threatening than having a conversation around my work and your work, and it's sort of a natural bridge to those dialogues.

-Joe, School Principal

Learning Cycles

"Innovation floats on a sea of inquiry, and curiosity is a driver for change." [119] Academic literature points to the importance of transforming inquiry into practice as a cornerstone of professional learning communities. "Teaching as inquiry" is a process that investigates the influence of teaching practices on student learning. It is intended to be designed as a cycle of set steps to show an improvement in student learning. Butler and Shnellert observe "Some of the most powerful learning occurs when teachers self-examine and engage in reflective inquiry cycles informed by assessment data." [120]

What does this process look like in practice? The principals in my study talked about this reflective inquiry and feedback process during their interviews. Joe spoke to the continual process of learning and how reflective, improvement cycles are a key to this process. The renewal process exists in a complex adaptive system, like those found in nature. This has significant implications for how a learning organization can use feedback loops to monitor, scan, detect errors, and then ultimately correct those errors.

Viewing the learning organization in this way provides the foundation for Timperley's teacher inquiry and knowledge-building cycle of professional learning. This model is structured around continuous feedback loops to promote important outcomes for students. Central to this self-regulatory process is the identification of a high-impact learning focus grounded in the learning needs of students. From this beginning, members of the professional learning organization establish goals for their learning and what they need to do, as professionals, to build their knowledge and skills.[121]

The next important feature of this feedback process is the clear use of evidence that guides professional learning in decision making: "A compelling and high leverage learning focus is based on evidence that it can have significant impact on teaching practices and student learning."[122] In seeing this iterative cycle of professional learning that will affect student learning as a function of continuous growth, once again, a return to the metaphor of ecology might be helpful. In the life of a living system, like the systems that exist in nature, an ongoing exchange with the environment is critical. This exchange—the life of a cycle of input, internal transformation, output, and feedback—influences subsequent cycles. In an open, living system, a self-regulating interdependence exists allowing for a steady state of balance to be maintained.[123]

Cycles of inquiry require ongoing evidence of learning be collected and acted

> What we've created is a feedback loop. We've done the same thing with our Educational Assistants' evaluations. We've created a feedback loop where it's not a one-time shot. Every time there was a walk through, we would stay depending on what they were doing. Sometimes a full block, sometimes it would transition into a second block; but then there would be a follow-up conversation, where we would talk about what we can celebrate from that, and what we can do better.
>
> **- Reia, School Principal**

upon. This means that decisions need to be made about what will be accepted as evidence, how frequently it will be collected, how it will be analyzed by the team and then what adjustments will be made to respond to the learners. Both Christine and Reia discussed their exploration of using evidence of student learning as key features of improvement cycles for their teachers. They acknowledged that they are beginning to work with these more flexible, adaptive processes. Cycles are intended to flow seamlessly based on responsiveness to what is going on for learners—the learner is at the centre.

Instead of waiting for the government to ask us to do these writing prompts, why don't we do it on a regular basis? And so just a few people tested it out last year. But now people are starting to say, why don't we because it's a great way to map out the kids' progress year to year. It's about people sitting down and saying let's examine student work, let's look at what's missing, let's build some goals around that.

- Christine, School Principal

The cycles of inquiry into practice are guided by questions about student learning that arise from investigation of the artifacts and demonstrations of student learning. They are fed forward through dialogue and shared curiosity about what teaching practices might lead to improvements among learners. Being open to learning, curious, and engaged in the continual learning and improvement of one's own professional practice requires a collective commitment to learning from and with each other; this is being lived out, in small and insightful ways, among the teachers experiencing leadership for learning in the schools of Reia, Christine, and Joe.

Have any of them found the silver bullet yet? Does a silver bullet even exist? Complex ecologies do not imply simple ideas or easy to apply solutions. Instead, complex ecologies suggest there will always be emerging and evolving approaches to understanding the interconnectedness of the parts, and that the whole can never be fully appreciated as a collection of individual, fragmented parts.

A helpful lens to look at the school, as an organization that learns, is described by using the term *not-yet-imaginable* to refer to the space of possibilities that exist in teaching and learning contexts. It is in this space, as described by researchers Davis and Sumara, where thoughts are not yet triggered:

So framed, the teacher is not only another learner within the classroom, but an integral part(icipant) within a grander learning system. Along with all the other individuals, the clusters of individuals...and the classroom collective as a whole, the teacher is teaching/learning. The teacher, that is, is constantly perturbating and being perturbated within the evolving, self-prompting system of the classroom collective.[124]

I suggest that the dialogue between the principals, me, and researchers exploring schools as complex ecological systems use the same lens to understand the experiences of leaders who wish to create schools that learn. According to Davis and Sumara, for school leaders in a complex world,

it is ridiculous to conceive of education in terms of top-down, ends-driven structures...[A]n education for the future is better understood as being oriented toward the as-yet unimagined—indeed, the currently unimaginable...[S]uch a goal can only be understood in terms of exploration of the current spaces of possibility.[125]

How do school leaders create a way of being, a school community that learns, that lives beyond the presence of the leader, the boss, the one controlling the school? Joe shared the words empowerment and ownership of learning not controlled by one individual, the leader, but instead, lives in every individual.

Is it conceivable that leaders might consider seeing challenges that confront them in the complex ecology of a school through new eyes? Might principals who wish to create a school community that learns together act differently in recognizing problems, obstacles, diverse learning needs, constant change and the demanding nature of living and learning in the twenty-first century as opportunities for moments of grace to be bestowed upon us and lead us to open up to a new way of being together where each new school year, month, day, and hour provides space for renewal?

For Reflection

Chapter Nine: Living the Questions

1. What do you do to contribute to a culture of inquiry within your school community? Within your school district?

2. Does your school community or school district have a shared understanding of what it means to be a qualified teacher? A qualified principal? A qualified superintendent?

3. What do you look for in a qualified teacher? A qualified principal? A qualified superintendent? Does this change over time and with the individual's experience?

4. In what ways do teachers, principals, district leaders reflect on their own growth and learning? How do they support each other's growth and learning?

5. Does your school community engage in iterative feedback cycles that guide teacher and student learning? Principal and school district leader learning? How is it structured and organized?

6. What constitutes evidence of success in student learning? In teacher learning? In principal and district leader learning? In your leadership? How is this evidence shared within the school community and beyond?

7. How often is evidence gathered? How does the school community adapt based on what the evidence suggests?

Conclusion

Dwelling in Possibility

Light comes from a flame lit from a spark,
This is who we are
And now, the end is where we start
I need a little symmetry,
a little bit of synergy,
a little bit of silence
This is who we are
I need a little symmetry,
a little bit of synergy,
a little bit of silence
The end is where we start

- my son, Ryan, "Boomerang"

The End is Where We Start

Are we creating school communities where all our learners can live up to a shared vision for student learning? The central problem to consider is a recognition that public schools are not evolving from an outdated, traditional factory-model approach to attend to students' learning. They are not changing in response to new developments and research on learning, the changing needs of today's learners, and changing societal needs.

I started chapter one with this assertion. Throughout the pages that followed, this thought guided me to shed a new light of understanding on how a principal's day-to-day practice of creating a school community that learns together might lead to renewed learning experiences for students so they can thrive in this changing world.

And now, *the end is where we start*. My son's song lyrics speak as I end this book. They once again remind me of where this all became not only a professional search for understanding, but also a deeply personal one. It was when the particular voice of one student, from one moment, captured in the song title this one student—my son—wrote in his grade 12 year: "Our Last Year as Cattle."

These words took hold of me in ways I could not comprehend until I came face-to-face with the philosophical art of interpretive inquiry within my doctoral program. I was hooked and drawn in to the mystery of Alethia, the unconcealment and concealment of the topic, that has been both intriguing and complex. My teachers, the philosophers, researchers, scholars—some I have met and others whom I have only engaged in conversation through their literature—have also guided my exploration: Gadamer, Greene, Davy, Jardine, Moules, McCaffrey, Field, Laing, and Friesen. Each contributed to opening up this new world of understanding for me. They drew me into the interpretive space of an intensely reflective research approach called hermeneutics. They offered an appreciation of hermeneutics as a way of being in and interpreting the world. They awakened within me the *magic of being addressed*.

Moules and her colleagues describe the hermeneutic research approach: Address, as experienced, can be a breathtaking and breath-sustaining gift. When it arrives, it asks that the researcher suffer the mysteries of the topic—and this means to put what they believe at risk, to be open to learning from risking what matters, and most importantly, to speak of this in human terms, to do well by "the tenants" that greet you at the portal. Thus, the servitude demanded by a topic is not primarily methodical, but rather ethical in nature…[I]t is a call of our conscience, that comes with an obligation to respond to the *call of what should be done*, and not simply, as in the natural sciences, what can be done.[126]

Reading my son's song title "Our Last Year as Cattle" again—14 years after it was originally written—stirred up something deep inside me. I re-awakened to what these words now suggested to me about my son's experience in school. The spark was re-ignited and an intense desire took hold to suffer the mysteries of the topic to uncover how leaders can lead schools while providing a different experience for their students. The sentiments shared by my son are not his alone. They are echoed in the voices of others as compiled by Friesen and Jardine in *21st-Century Learners Speak Out On 21st-Century Learning:*

- We want to do work that makes a difference to me and to my world.
- We don't want to remember, recall, and regurgitate.
- We don't want to learn for the sake of tests.
- We don't want learning made easy; rather, we want it to mean something.
- We want to learn with the media of our times.
- We want to do work that is relevant, meaningful, and authentic.
- We want to be engaged intellectually.
- We want stronger relationships with teachers, with each other and with communities locally, provincially, nationally, and globally.
- We want teachers to know how we learn, to take into account what we understand and what we misunderstand, and use this knowledge as a starting place to guide our continued learning.
- We want to be able to work with others in the classroom, online and in our community.
- We want to be able to pick up our information anywhere, anytime.
- We want in-depth learning.
- We need feedback in time to help us learn and in time to do something about it.[127]

The end is where we start, and we must always start with the student. At every level in the system, starting with the student and keeping the student in focus requires a commitment to practicing powerful pedagogy that enlivens the learning for our students in ways that see them thrive in this changing world.

Research tells us that school leadership is the second most important in-school factor that predicts student outcomes, after quality of teaching.[128] Guided by this understanding, the school principal who wishes to create a school community that learns together is responsible for creating the conditions that directly affect learning for all members of the school community.

This book has explored school principls' practical experience in creating school communities that learn so the understandings might contribute to current research around school leadership that shapes and is shaped by the interconnected landscapes of continuous change. Understanding the complexity of social collectives such as the school community, it is not a matter of seeking facts to answer the question "What is?" nor is it only the interpretation-seeking "What might be?" Instead, it is a practice-oriented question that asks, "How should we act?"[129]

Three compelling topics—being open, creating fertile ground, and engaging in cycles of renewal—previously hidden from me, were opened up, unconcealed, through conversations with principals Christine, Joe, and Reia; from my own leadership journey; and from numerous deep dives into the existing research literature. The topics called out to me in particular ways during extended periods of silence when reflection allowed me to understand the synergy between my own journey; the experiences of the three principals; the broader, global, research I investigated; and the words and messages of poets, teachers, and writers. It was in the back-and-forth movement among these rich sources of information that I discovered a case for a new and different understanding woven together from these three topics.

When taken together, these ideas create symmetry through an interconnected wholeness. This integrated understanding illuminates a possible future for renewed leadership practice that answers the question "How should we act?" so that an enlivened educational future for students can emerge.

A Future is Struggling to Emerge

Making way for a new and different future struggling to emerge requires a new and different way of being in the world. Melody Beattie reminds us: "Open to life's abundance. Open to all its possibilities. The more open you become, the more creative you'll be…the more creative you are, the more possibilities you'll see." [130] A way of being that is both an awakening and a deepening of understanding of how one learns of new possibilities that "break the cotton wool of habit" [131] is suggested by Greene.

With the works of Greene and others as my guide, I attended to three topics in new ways, causing me to "think what we are doing." [132] This way of thinking provides an opportunity to detach from the routine patterns of what one does. This frees us to reflect on just what might be the obstacle that is creating the problem. It is through noticing problems, or things being not right, that one can become open to a new way of acting. In her book *Dialectic of Freedom*, Maxine Greene describes this process:

> For Jean-Paul Sartre, the project of acting on our freedom involves a rejection of the unsufficient or the unendurable, a clarification, an imaging of a better state of things….Made conscious of lacks, they may move (in their desire to repair them) toward a "field of possibles," what is possible or realizable for them…For Sartre, they do not reach out for fulfillment if they do not feel impeded somehow, and if they are not enabled to name the obstacles that stand in their way. At once, the very existence of obstacles depends on the desire to reach toward wider spaces for fulfillment, to expand options, to know alternatives. As has been said, a rock is an obstacle only to the one who wants to climb the hill. Not caring, the traveller merely takes another path. He/she is like the gentleman Dostoevsky described in *Notes from Underground*, who comes up against a stone wall and simply stops. "For these people a wall is not the challenge that it is for people like you and me who think…it is not an excuse to turn back" [133]

Moules and her colleagues point out that "practitioners *suffer these things in their practice*" (emphasis in the original text) and it is through the suffering—

that recognition of a problem or challenge that an obstacle, an entrenched, rutted, outdated routine or structure may be uncovered. This makes it possible to "break the cotton wool of habit": to envision new and better ways to act and bring something new into being. To make this possible, one must orient toward being open to the future.

> Although education often means the ceaseless proliferation of longer and longer lists, guides, schedules, and agenda, at its heart, it cannot be caught in the stasis that such a tendency requires and desires in the end. Rather, education is ek-static, a movement beyond what already is, a reaching out to the new life around us in a way that keeps open the possibility "that the people of this precious Earth…may live."[134]

Bumping up against the challenges and obstacles uncovered through this process stimulated in me an emergent understanding, a new lens as it were, through which I viewed problems and obstacles. I now saw the possibility of a different future struggling to emerge. I formed a new understanding about how principals could act in ways that require them to behold the Open and create fertile ground, leading to renewal. This answers the call of what can and should be done.

The words of poet Rainer Maria Rilke spoke to me of an imposed way of being in the world: ordered, contrived, and controlled.

> With their whole gaze
> Animals behold the Open.
> Only our eyes
> are as though reversed
> and set like traps around us,
> keeping us inside.

I became aware of a more natural and wholesome orientation to this world; a foundational understanding emerged. As my kindred spirits, the practicing principals spoke about the organic nature of authentic, powerful learning they observed among their teachers and other staff and encountered in the day-to-day practice of teaching, I connected with a new metaphor for learning and a re-imagined structure for today's schools that offers the possibility for a new future. This new metaphor draws on complexity thinking to create an ecological paradigm, recognizing wholeness and interconnectivity as it exists in nature. It requires openness to what comes to us, what addresses us, before imposing rigid structures. Greene describes these rigid structures as

> artificial barriers erected in the way of children trying to create authentic selves....All have, as has been said before, to be perceived as obstacles, most often obstacles erected by other human beings (sometimes, but not always, in complicity with the self involved), if freedom is to be achieved.[135]

When leaders can see interconnectedness, they can better understand the controls that were imposed: controls that do not respond to the organic natural flow of life lived in the dynamic, complex social setting of a school. By becoming a critical observer of their schools, leaders create opportunities to distance themselves from the day-to-day routines. They see their school communities with new eyes—eyes that become focused on their lively and dynamic communities in a natural, ecological way. From this different viewpoint, a new vista opens up.

This expanded, spacious vista provides principals and teacher leaders with new freedom to open up to natural moments for authentic learning and problem solving. New opportunities are possible to break free of outdated mechanistic structures that keep schools bound and burdened, constricted and compressed by remnant routines and processes from an industrialized era. These rutted routines have become deadwood in today's modern, dynamic, and complex schools.

What does this understanding mean for school leaders who wish to create a school community that learns together? In what ways do teachers and administrators respond to the call of *what should be done*? Rumi offers this in his poem "A Great Wagon":

Out beyond ideas of wrongdoing and rightdoing,
there is a field. I'll meet you there.

These lines from Rumi's poem speak to a particular way that learners come together in a school community that learns together. It conjures up an image of an open space, a field, a meeting place free from judgment. It is a space where openness to dialogue is expected and challenges are viewed not as disruptions to the work but as opportunities to clear space and make way for the new. This vision of a possible future for schools that learn together requires intentional actions and an open-to-learning disposition by the school principal. It is not easy to cultivate the fertile ground needed for this way of coming together, however.

An orientation toward an ecological metaphor recognizes the co-evolutionary adaptive environment that exists not only in the complex relationships found in nature, but also in the social settings of schools that learn. With this orientation, principals may act in ways that demonstrate their understanding of the importance of building high relational trust within their school community. Building relational trust means respect for valuing the ideas of others, personal regard, competence, and integrity. It is crucial in creating fertile ground for teachers to open up to learn from and with each other, free from judgment. Within this environment, learning is enacted among smaller teams or clusters that understand the important contributions and influence of a collective of individuals. According to Greene:

> It is clear enough that choice and action both occur within and by means of ongoing transactions with objective conditions and with other human beings. Whatever is chosen and acted upon must be grounded, at least to a degree, in an awareness of a world lived in common with others, a world that can be to some extent transformed.[136]

The creation of fertile ground provides objective conditions for choice and action with other human beings; it is grounded in an awareness of a world lived in common with others. Within this natural setting, one of interconnectedness, both leaders and teachers will find it possible to tap into their natural, innate curiosity to grow. They will get better at creating space to address problems and challenges and will be exposed to alternative new ways of learning together. This requires principals to act in new and different ways: they will need to model openness and vulnerability as a learner among others while still maintaining high expectations for continuous growth and improvement.

Christine, Reia, and Joe all shared experiences that surfaced their commitment to being learners and their willingness to walk beside their teachers. They intentionally notice opportunities for job-embedded contextual learning that happens in the situated, natural moments of the day-to-day life within their schools. These three principals are living examples of what it means to enact professional leadership practices that contribute to the advancement of a learning community. The recently approved Professional Practice Standard for Leaders in Alberta calls for principals to develop competencies of fostering effective relationships, leading a learning community, and developing leadership capacity. The document suggests that leaders will achieve competence according to indicators such as engaging in collegial relationships while modelling and promoting open collaborative dialogue, nurturing and sustaining evidence-informed teaching, developing a shared responsibility for the success of all students, and engaging in team building and shared leadership. However, this document falls short. It does not provide principals and leaders with a deeper understanding about not only what they must *know* but what they must *do* and how they must *be* to become competent in these areas.

New understandings have surfaced about building relational trust and decentralizing the role of the leader so leadership encompasses more than just sharing tasks or a doling out responsibilities to be checked off the list. Instead, this new understanding calls for a leadership collective that leads learning for and with each other.

The imperative to create fertile ground recognizes the influence of school leaders on teachers; school leaders either constrain or enable teachers' daily practice. Effective leaders build cultures where effective educators can change their routine professional practices and learn to improve student outcomes. Fertile ground creates opportunities for the neighboring cross-pollination of people and their ideas, making it possible for more educators to use their expertise to elevate the capabilities of colleagues across a school or a system.[137] Establishing fertile ground of this nature cultivates the possibility for understanding how leadership might be enacted differently. This new vision for the practice of leadership exists in the interactions between and among individuals in schools, rather than as embodied in a particular role or title.

My research uncovered the day to day leadership practices of three school leaders who demonstrate it is possible to create fertile ground. Christine, Joe, and Reia are principals activating networks of leaders throughout their school communities "to truly increase the teaching and learning capacity of a school [so that] more people…have the knowledge, judgment and skills required to shape and guide learning."[138]

And principals who wish to create schools that learn together might learn to recognize that it is not enough to cultivate openness to new ways of being together in schools; they must also understand that their leadership requires that they nurture engagement in an ever-changing process of continual renewal. As Maya Angelou tells us:

> Each new hour holds new chances
> for new beginnings.
> Do not be wedded forever
> to fear, yoked eternally
> to brutishness.

What needs to happen to simultaneously hold onto that which the past can offer while realizing some things need to die so the new can emerge? Within this renewal process, leaders are called on to merge their disposition for openness, letting go of traditional organization structures of control to take up their responsibility to create fertile ground. Within this renewed context, new processes can be developed to promote ongoing inquiry into practice: gather evidence, adjust practices to new learning, gather more evidence, mediate communally through open-to-learning conversations, and allow the new to emerge with a decentralized network of learners. The leader who shows up with this disposition toward continuous improvement and adaptive learning will become competent in living a commitment to professional learning. Creating a school community that learns together is possible when leaders engage in learning with others by actively, as the Alberta Standard phrases it, "seeking out feedback and information to enhance leadership practices" and "seeking, critically reviewing and applying educational research to inform effective practice."[139] Leaders who establish such collaborative knowledge-building processes within their school communities can establish renewal that opens up the possibility for continuous improvement in a constantly changing, increasingly complex world.

What can be understood differently and ultimately acted upon through a new understanding of renewal? Most important, the experience of leading a school community that learns together cannot be reduced to checking off a list of skills. It requires ongoing practice and experiences within the day-to-day context of a busy, complex school community. It must be enacted among collaborative networks where space and time are prioritized for meeting, in school community and around the work. The observations, products, and conversations that are collected are evidence to address collective development of solutions to challenges and problems of practice—solutions explored, tested, and assessed in an ongoing cyclical inquiry process. A leader oriented toward renewal within their school community will create opportunities for professional learning time spent working through action research cycles, allowing leaders and teachers to productively learn together in renewing their practice.

With fresh eyes that come from the deeply reflective process I engaged in most recently through my research, I see differently, I appreciate differently, and I understand differently. From this space, I dwell—with others, researchers, writers, poets, philosophers, song writers, teachers, and principals—in possibility. This space of possibility starts and ends with an ethical call for action to be taken to better serve our students, our hope for the future. Educators have an obligation to ensure that students within our classrooms and schools do not find themselves, at the end of grade 12, eager for a much-anticipated and long-awaited release from "Our Last Year as Cattle." We can and must do better for our children.

This call for action is needed to awaken within our teachers a renewed and deeper understanding of what it means to create the conditions for students to engage in authentic learning experiences. This can only occur within a collaborative learning community that nurtures individual and collective growth. Effective teaching practices spread by school leaders across classrooms, corridors, school communities, and districts create the conditions for teachers to engage in being together differently. This inspired leadership answers the question *How should we act?*

Is it possible, within a renewed leadership model, that a networked system of leaders could courageously respond to an ethical call, a call of our conscience, that comes with an obligation to respond to the call of what should be done?

Might this ethical call replace naïve compliance to tightly prescribed, simplistically understood competencies within a Professional Practice Standard such as the cattle drive for principals in Alberta, which has been assumed to constitute a once-and-for-all truth about school leadership?

Is this possible? Can today's school leaders create conditions within their schools that will see responsive, growth-oriented, adaptive learning communities thrive? I take hope from the poem "I Dwell in Possibility" by poet Emily Dickinson:

> I dwell in Possibility –
> A fairer House than Prose –
> More numerous of Windows –
> Superior – for Doors –
> Of Chambers as the Cedars –
> Impregnable of eye –
> And for an everlasting Roof
> The Gambrels of the Sky –
> Of Visitors – the fairest –
> For Occupation – This –
> The spreading wide my narrow Hands
> To gather Paradise –

September 2020

Today I open my laptop to a space I created for my book manuscript. I have been dreaming about this for as long as I can remember. I am reading my work over, one more time, before I send my first draft to my editor. I am a WRITER!

Parent, Teacher, Principal, Researcher, and now Writer; living out these roles over the past 35 years has shaped my way of looking at our existing educational system. Through my lived experiences in these roles, I developed a deeper understanding for the extraordinary that lives within the ordinary day-to-day moments of a school day, that make up a school year, that have made up 35 years of my life. I have felt the joy of connecting with learners, both students and colleagues, and witnessing the spark of curiosity that comes alive when the conditions for learning have been created. I have also felt disappointment, heartache, and frustration when the love of learning has been extinguished—when students and those who teach them are no longer engaged in learning that matters.

This is an ordinary, yet extraordinary, moment. I've extended to you an invitation to dwell in possibility: the possibility of renewal. The ground is fertile, ready to release today's leaders to become different. In this new context, leaders whose curious, questioning, and thoughtful way of being with others as explorers, insatiable learners, and warriors are poised to open up to not only envisioning a renewed future, in all its possibilities, but also to becoming the authors, designers, and choreographers of this future.

Endnotes

Introduction | Leaving the Old for the New

1   Moules, McCaffrey, Field, & Laing (2015, p. 180).

Part One | Room to Breathe

Opening Poem: The Open, from Rainer Maria Rilke's *Eighth Duino Elegy* (2005).

2   Jardine (2016, p. 65).

Chapter One | Behold the Open

3   Taylor (1911).

4   Davey (2006/2012, p. xv).

5   Erickson (2018, p. 59).

6   Pinar (2008, p. 134).

7   Galef (1998).

8   Friesen, & Jardine (2009, p. 14).

9   Online Etymology Dictionary (2020).

10   Ibid.

11   Eisner (1998, p. 213).

12   Senge (2006).

13   Greene (1988).

14   Davis, & Sumara (2007, p. 62).

Chapter Two | Being Open

15   Perkins (2014, p. 8).

16   Barrie (2015, p. 172).

17   Clifford, & Marinucci (2008, p. 680).

18   Moules, McCaffrey, Field, & Laing (2015, p. 52).

19   Davey (2006/2012, p. 59).

20   Ibid., p. xvi.

21   Redfield (1993, p. 169).

22   Muth (2002, p. 26).

23   Davis, Sumara, & Luce-Kapler (2000, p. 65).

24   Eisner (1998, p. 111).

25   Berger (2014, p. 76).

26   Singer (2007, p. 45).

27   Csikszentmihalyi, M. (1990).

Chapter Three | Openings

28   Caputo (1987, p. 177).

29   Hallinger (2012, p. 9).

30   Lynch (2012, p. 30).

31   Scherer (2003, p. 5).

32   Fullan (2014, p. 45).

33   Blasé, & Blasé (1998, p. 14).

34   Brandon, Friesen, Koh, Parsons, Adams, Mombourquette, Hunter, & Stelmach (2018, p. 38).

35   Tolle (2006, p. 194–195).

Part Two | Fertile Ground

Opening Poem: The mystic Sufi poet Rumi wrote these lines in the thirteenth century in his poem *A Great Wagon* (Youssef, 2016).

36   Online Etymology Dictionary (2020).

37   Josselson (2013, p. 9).

38   Thich Nhat Hanh (1991, p. 78–79).

Chapter Four | A Different Way to be Together

39   Educational researchers Ash & D'Auria (2013); Bryk & Schneider (2002); Friesen, Jacobsen, Brown, & Yanez (2016); Robinson (2011); Shapiro & Permuth (2013); and Timperley (2011) all write about the importance of trust in a learning organization.

40   Palmer (2004).

41   Tschannen-Moran, & Gareis (2015, p. 69).

42   Wood (2001, p. 3–4).

43   Online Etymology Dictionary (2020).

44   Palmer (2004, p. 16).

45   Ibid., p. 17.

46   Online Etymology Dictionary (2020).

47   Covey (2008, p. 145).

48   Brown (2012, p. 185).

49   Ibid., p. 199.

50   Frankl (2006).

51   Palmer (2004, p. 109).

52   Brandon, Friesen, Koh, Parsons, Adams, Mombourquette, Hunter, & Stelmach (2018, p. 189).

53   Coelho (2014).

54   Robinson (2019).

55   Little (1987, p. 493).

Chapter Five | Feeding Off Each Other

56   Lambert (2002, p. 37).

57   Berry (2012, p. 61).

58   Bransford, Brown, & Cocking (2000).

59   Mourshed, Chijioke, & Barber (2010, p. 4).

60   Breakspear, Peterson, Alfadala, & Khair (2017, p. 3).

61 Timperley (2011, p. 107).

62 Beattie (1996, p. 315–316).

63 Rilke (1984).

64 Capra (1996, p. 290).

65 Ibid., p. 291.

66 Redfield (1993, p. 215).

67 Ritchhart (2015, p. 4).

68 Educational researchers Hung, Lee, & Lim (2012); Lombardi (2007); Newmann, Marks & Gamoran (1996); Newmann, Bryk & Nagaoka (2001); and Scardamalia & Bereiter (2006) all write about the principles of authentic learning.

69 Capra (1996, p. 291).

70 Ibid., p. 294.

71 Greene (1978, p. 81).

72 Greene (1988, p. 17).

73 Ibid.

Part Three | Renewal

Opening Poem: *On the Pulse of Morning* by Maya Angelou, written for US President Bill Clinton's inauguration in 1993.

Chapter Six | Networks of Influence

74 Online Etymology Dictionary (2020).

75 Schleicher (2015, p. 61).

76 Ibid.

77 Organization for Economic Cooperation and Development. (2015, p. 104).

78 Bakkenes, Vermunt, & Wubbels (2010).

79 Timperley, Kaser, & Halbert (2014, p. 4).

80 Organization for Economic Cooperation and Development. (2015, p. 18).

81 Jardine (2016, p. 33).

82 Ibid., p. 13.

83 Gadamer (1960/1989, p. xxiv).

84 Jardine (2016, p. 40).

85 Gadamer (1983, p. 110–111).

86 Davis, & Sumara (2006, p. xvii).

87 Friesen, & Jardine (2009, p. 5).

88 Jardine, Clifford, & Friesen (2008, p. 14).

89 Friesen, & Jardine (2009, p. 5).

90 Bransford, Brown, & Cocking (2000).

91 Jardine, & Friesen (2013, p. 30).

92 Kanigel (2005, p. 19).

93 Wrege, & Greenwood (1991, p. xx).

94 Hallinger (2012, p. 9).

95 Timperley, & Earl (2012, p. 6).

96 Carmichael, & Hadžikadić (2019).

97 Jardine (2016, p. 298).

98 Capra (1996, p. 6).

99 Ted Perry, inspired by Chief Seattle; taken from Capra (1996, p. xi).

100 Davis, & Sumara (2006, p. 70).

101 Surowiecki (2004, p. 161).

102 Davis, & Sumara (2006).

Chapter Seven | Collective Leadership

103 Online Etymology Dictionary (2020).

104 Davis, & Sumara (2006, p. 142).

105 Ibid., p. 143.

106   Ibid., p. 144.

107   Capra (1996, p. 27).

108   Schnellert, & Butler (2014).

109   Wilson, & Wilson (2000, p. 11–12).

110   Doll (2008, p. 193).

Chapter Eight | Spreading Seeds

111   Montgomery (1908, p. 138).

112   Davis, Sumara, & Luce-Kapler (2000, p. 71).

113   Davis, & Sumara (2006, p. 92).

114   Kelley, & Kelley (2013).

115   Senge (1999, p. 43).

116   Capra (1996, p. 7).

Chapter Nine | Living the Questions

Opening Poem: *On Questions* by Rainer Maria Rilke (1984).

117   Montgomery (1908, p. 15).

118   Alberta Government. (2015, January 1).

119   Timperley, Kaser, & Halbert (2014, p. 4).

120   Butler, & Schnellert (2012, p. 1206).

121   Timperley (2011, p. 11).

122   Earl & Timperley (2012, p. 12).

123   Vornberg (2013, p. 807).

124   Davis, & Sumara (2007, p. 62).

125   Davis, & Sumara (2006, p. 135).

Conclusion | Dwelling in Possibility

126   Moules, McCaffrey, Field, & Laing (2014, p. 2).

127   Friesen, & Jardine (2009, p. 3).

128   Louis, Leithwood, Wahlstrom, & Anderson (2010).

129   Davis, & Sumara (2006, p. 25).

130   Beattie (1996, p. 74).

131   Greene (1988, p. 2).

132   Arendt (1958, p. 5).

133   Greene (1988, p. 5).

134   Fox (1983, p. 9).

135   Greene (1988, p. 9).

136   Ibid., p. 4.

137   Ibid., p. 28.

138   Ibid., p. 25.

139   Alberta Education. (2018).

Ending Poem: *I Dwell in Possibility*, by Emily Dickinson (Franklin, 1999).

Bibliography

Alberta Education. (2018). *Leadership quality standard*. Alberta Government.

Alberta Government. (2015, January 1). *Teacher growth, supervision, and evaluation policy (TGSEP)*. https://open.alberta.ca/publications/teacher-growth-supervision-and-evaluation-policy.

Angelou, M. (1993, January 21). The Inauguration: Maya Angelou: "On the Pulse of Morning." *The New York Times*, National edition, p. A00014.

Arendt, H. (1958). *The human condition*. University of Chicago Press.

Ash, P. B., & D'Auria, J. (2013). Blueprint for a Learning System: Create One Larger, More Flexible Team That Encourages Collaboration in All Directions. *Journal of Staff Development, 34*(3), 42–46.

Bakkenes, I., Vermunt, J. D., & Wubbels, T. (2010). Teacher learning in the context of educational innovation: Learning activities and learning outcomes of experienced teachers. *Learning and Instruction, 20*(6), 533–548.

Barrie, J. M. (2015). *Peter Pan*. Printers Row Publishing Group.

Beattie, M. L. (1996). *Journey to the heart: Daily meditations on the path to freeing your soul*. HarperCollins.

Berger, W. (2014). *A more beautiful question: The power of inquiry to spark breakthrough ideas*. Bloomsbury Publishing.

Berry, Wendell (2012). *The long-legged house*. Counterpoint.

Blasé, J., & Blasé, J. (1998). *Handbook of instructional leadership: How really good principals promote teaching and learning*. Corwin Press.

Brandon, J., Friesen, S., Koh, K., Parsons, D., Adams, P., Mombourquette, C., Hunter, D., & Stelmach, B. (2018). *Building, supporting, and assuring quality professional practice*. A report prepared for Alberta Education.

Bransford, J. D., Brown, A. L., & Cocking, R. R. (2000). *How people learn: Brain, mind, experience, and school*. National Academy Press.

Breakspear. S., Peterson, A., Alfadala, A., & Khair, B.M. (2017). Executive summary of the research findings. *Developing agile leaders of learning: School leadership policy for dynamic times*. WISE Qatar Foundation.

Brown, B. (2012). *Daring greatly: How the courage to be vulnerable transforms the way we live, love, parent and lead*. Penguin Group.

Bryk, A. S., & Schneider, B. (2002). *Trust in schools: A core resource for improvement*. Russell Sage Foundation.

Butler, D. L., & Schnellert, L. (2012). Collaborative inquiry in teacher professional development. *Teaching and Teacher Education: An International Journal of Research and Studies, 28*(8), 1206–1220.

Capra, F. (1996). *The web of life: A new understanding of living systems*. Anchor Books.

Caputo, J. (1987). *Radical hermeneutics*. Indiana University Press.

Carmichael, T. & Hadžikadić, M. (2019). The fundamentals of complex adaptive systems. In T. Carmichael, A. J. Collins, & M. Hadžikadić (Eds.), *Complex adaptive systems: Understanding complex systems* (pp. 1–16). Springer, Cham. Retrieved November 21, 2020, from https://link.springer.com/book/10.1007/978-3-030-20309-2_1.

Clifford, P., & Marinucci, S. (2008). Voices inside schools: testing the waters: Three elements of classroom inquiry. *Harvard Educational Review, 78*(4), 675–688.

Coelho, P. (2014). *The alchemist* (25th anniversary ed.). HarperCollins Publishers, Inc.

Covey, S. (2008). *The speed of trust.* Free Press.

Csikszentmihalyi, M. (1990). *Flow: The psychology of optimal experience.* Harper & Row.

Davey, N. (2006/2012). *Unquiet understanding: Gadamer's philosophical hermeneutics.* SUNY Press.

Davis, B., & Sumara, D. (2006). *Complexity and education: Inquiries into learning, teaching and research.* Lawrence Erlbaum Associates Inc.

Davis, B., & Sumara, D. (2007). Complexity science and education: Reconceptualizing the teacher's role in learning. *Interchange, 38*(1), 53–63.

Davis, B., Sumara, D., & Luce-Kapler, R. (2000). *Engaging minds: Learning and teaching in a complex world.* Lawrence Erlbaum Associates.

Doll, W. E. (2008). Complexity and the culture of curriculum. *Educational Philosophy and Theory, 40*(1).

Earl, L., & Timperley H. (2012). *Learning and change networks: A background paper on designing networks to make a difference.* Faculty of Education, The University of Auckland.

Eisner, E. W. (1998). *The kind of schools we need: Personal essays.* Heinemann.

Erickson, F. in Denzin, N.K. & Lincoln, Y.S. (2018). *The Sage Handbook of Qualitative Research* (5th ed.). Sage.

Fox, M. (1983). *Original blessing.* Bear and Company.

Frankl, V. (2006). *Man's search for meaning.* Beacon Press.

Franklin, R. W. (Ed.)(1999). *The Poems of Emily Dickinson.* Harvard University Press.

Friesen, S., & Jardine, D. (2009). *21st-century learning and learners: A report prepared for western and northern Canadian curriculum protocol.* Galileo Educational Network.

Friesen, S., Jacobsen, M., Brown, B., & Alonso Yanez, G. (2016). *Highly adaptive learning systems: Research in seven redesigned high schools in Alberta.* Alberta Education. Retrieved from http://abhsredesign.ca/wp-content/uploads/2016/05/High-School-Redesign-Research-2016.pdf.

Fullan, M. (2014). *The principal: Three keys to maximizing impact.* Jossey-Bass.

Gadamer, H-G. (1960/1989). *Truth and method* (2nd rev. ed.) (J. Weinsheimer & D.G. Marshall, Trans.). Continuum.

Gadamer, H-G. (1983). *Reason in the age of science.* MIT Press.

Galef, B. G. (1998). Edward Thorndike: Revolutionary psychologist, ambiguous biologist. *American Psychologist, 53*(10), 1128–1134.

Greene, M. (1978). *Landscapes of learning.* Teachers College Press.

Greene, M. (1988). *The dialectic of freedom.* Teachers College Press.

Hallinger, P. (2012). Leadership for 21st century schools: From instructional leadership to leadership for learning. In P. Hallinger, *School leadership that makes a difference: Lessons from 30 years of international research.* The Hong Kong Institute of Education. https://silo.tips/download/lessons-from-30-years-of-international-research.

Hung, D., Lee, S. S., & Lim, K. Y. (2012). Authenticity in learning for the twenty-first century: Bridging the formal and the informal. *Educational Technology Research and Development, 60*(6), 1071–1091.

Jardine, D. W. (2016). *In praise of radiant beings: A retrospective path through education, Buddhism, and ecology.* Information Age Publishing.

Jardine, D., & Friesen, S. (2013). Implementation guide: Guiding principles for WNCP curriculum framework projects. DOI: 10.131400/RG.2.217894.47682.

Jardine, D., Clifford, P., & Friesen, S. (2008). *Back to the basics of teaching and learning: Thinking the world together* (2nd ed.). Erlbaum.

Josselson, R. (2013). *Interviewing for qualitative inquiry: A relational approach.* Guilford Press.

Kanigel, R. (2005). *The one best way: Fredrick Winslow Taylor and the enigma of efficiency.* MIT Press.

Kelley, T., & Kelley, D. (2013). *Creative confidence: Unleashing the creative confidence within us all.* Harper Collins Publishers.

Lambert, L. (2002). A framework for shared leadership. *Educational Leadership, 59*(8), 37–40.

Little, J. W. (1987). Teachers as colleagues. In. V. Richardson-Koehler (ed.), *Educator's handbook.* Longman.

Lombardi, M. M. (2007). Authentic learning for the 21st century: An overview. *Educause learning initiative, 1,* 1–12.

Louis, K. S., Leithwood, K., Wahlstrom, K. L., & Anderson, S.E. et al. (2010). *Learning from leadership project: Final report of research to the Wallace Foundation.* University of Minnesota.

Lynch, M. (2012). *A guide to effective school leadership theories.* Routledge.

Montgomery, L. M. (1908). *Anne of Green Gables.* London Seal Books.

Moules, N. J., McCaffrey, G., Field, J. C., & Laing, C. M. (2014). Conducting hermeneutic research: The address of the topic. *Journal of Applied Hermeneutics, April 23, 2014*(Article 7).

Moules, N.J., McCaffrey, G., Field, J.C., & Laing, C. (2015). *Conducting hermeneutic research: From philosophy to practice.* Peter Lang.

Mourshed, M., Chijioke, C. & Barber, M. (2010). *How the world's most improved school systems keep getting better.* McKinsey & Company.

Muth, J. J. (2002). *The three questions.* Scholastic Press.

Newmann, F. M., Bryk, A. S., & Nagaoka, J. K. (2001). *Improving Chicago's schools: Authentic intellectual work and standardized tests: Conflict or coexistence?* Consortium on Chicago School Research.

Newman, F. M., Marks, H. M., & Gamoran, A. (1996). Authentic pedagogy and student performance. *American Journal of Education, 104*(4), 280–312.

Online Etymology Dictionary | Origin, history and meaning of English words (2020). Retrieved from https://www.etymonline.com/.

Organization for Economic Cooperation and Development. (2015). *Schooling redesigned: Towards innovative learning systems, educational research and innovation.* OECD.

Palmer, P. (2004). *A hidden wholeness: The journey towards an undivided life.* Jossey-Bass.

Perkins, D. (2014). *Future wise: Educating our children for a changing world.* Jossey-Bass.

Pinar, W. (2008). Introduction to a common countenance. *Journal of the Canadian Association for Curriculum Studies, 6*(2), 129–155.

Redfield, J. (1993). *The celestine prophecy.* Warner Books Inc.

Rilke, R.M. (1984). *Letters to a young poet.* Translated by Stephen Mitchell. Random House.

Rilke, R. M., Barrows, A., Macy, J., & Rilke, R. M. (2005). *In praise of mortality: Selections from Rilke's duino elegies and sonnets to orpheus.* Riverhead Books.

Ritchhart, R. (2015). *Creating cultures of thinking: The 8 forces we must master to truly transform our schools.* Jossey-Bass.

Robinson, V. (2011). *Student-centred leadership.* Jossey-Bass.

Robinson, V. (2019). *Open-to-learning conversations: Background paper* [unpublished manuscript]. The University of Auckland.

Scardamalia, M., & Bereiter, C. (2006). Knowledge building: Theory, pedagogy, and technology. In K. Sawyer (Ed.), *Cambridge handbook of the learning sciences* (pp. 97–118). New York: Cambridge University Press.

Scherer, M. (2003). *Keeping good teachers.* Association for Supervision and Curriculum Development.

Schleicher, A. (2015). *Schools for 21st-century learners: Strong leaders, confident teachers, innovative approaches.* Organization for Economic Cooperation and Development (OECD).

Schnellert, L., & Butler, D. L. (2014). Collaborative inquiry: Empowering teachers in their professional development. *Education Canada, 54*(3), 42–44.

Senge, P. M. (2006). *The fifth discipline: The art & practice of the learning organization.* Doubleday.

Senge, P.M. (1999). *The dance of change: the challenges of sustaining momentum in learning organizations.* Currency/Doubleday.

Shapiro, A., & Permuth, S. (2013). Organizational theory in light of constructivist thinking. In B. Irby (Ed.), *Handbook of educational theories* (pp. 855–869). Information Age Publishing.

Singer, M. A. (2007). *The untethered soul: The journey beyond yourself.* New Harbinger Publications.

Surowiecki, J. (2004). *The wisdom of crowds: why the many are stronger than the few and how collective wisdom shapes business, economies, societies, and nations.* Doubleday.

Taylor, F. W. (1911). *The principles of scientific management.* Harper & Brothers.

Thich Nhat Hanh (1991). *Peace is every step.* Bantam Books.

Timperley, H. (2011). *Realizing the power of professional learning.* McGraw Hill, Open University Press.

Timperley, H., Kaser, L., & Halbert, J. (2014). *A framework for transforming learning in schools: Innovation and the spiral of inquiry.* (Seminar series paper No. 234). Centre for Strategic Education https://www.educationalleaders.govt.nz/Pedagogy-and-assessment/Evidence-based-leadership/The-spiral-of-inquiry.

Timperley, H., & Earl, L. (2012). *Learning and change networks: A background paper on designing networks to make a difference.* Faculty of Education, The University of Auckland.

Tolle, E. (2006). *A new earth: Awakening to your life's purpose.* Penguin Group.

Tschannen-Moran, M., & Gareis, C.R., (2015). Faculty trust in the principal: an essential ingredient in high-performing schools. *Journal of Educational Administration, 53(1),* 66–92.

Vornberg, J. A. (2013). Systems theory. In B. Irby (Ed.), *Handbook of educational theories.* Information Age Publishing.

Wilson, P., & Wilson, S. (2000). Circles in the classroom: The cultural significance of structure. *Canadian Social Studies, 34*(2), 11–12.

Wood, D. (2001). *Fawn island.* University of Minnesota Press.

Wrege, C. D., & Greenwood, R. (1991). *Frederick W. Taylor: The father of scientific management: Myth and reality.* Irwin Professional Publishing.

Youssef, A. (2016, December 12). The Rumi poem we should all read. [Blog post]. Retrieved from https://www.elephantjournal.com/2016/12/the-rumi-poem-we-should-all-read.

About the Author

Carolyn Cameron EdD is an educator with over 30 years of experience within the K–12 public school system. Her career began as a teacher working with the most difficult to reach students who demonstrated both behavioural and learning challenges. It was from this humble beginning that she recognized success for her students would only be achieved when she drew on the contributions from a team of professionals to create a responsive, adaptive classroom community. Carolyn deepened her commitment to teamwork when she co-created a "one room schoolhouse" where she and her colleagues shared students and a large, flexibly designed teaching space that would engage young children in project-based learning. Later, as an administrator of a new middle school, Carolyn brought with her the profoundly powerful learning from her team teaching experiences to her new role as a school leader.

Carolyn has presented at local, provincial, national and international conferences on the power of collaboration to lead meaningful student learning within a school community. As a school principal, she was nominated twice and was a recipient of a provincial excellence in teaching award. A lifelong learner, Carolyn recently earned her Doctor of Education degree from the University of Calgary. Carolyn's professional experience includes serving as a leadership consultant for Alberta Education and Galileo Educational Network. Currently, when Carolyn is not traveling with her husband, she works as a sessional instructor for school leadership programs at the University of Calgary and the University of Lethbridge.

CPSIA information can be obtained
at www.ICGtesting.com
Printed in the USA
BVHW061312240321
603332BV00004B/474

9 781777 210700